SOUTHERN REGION THROUGH THE 1970s

Year By Year

MICHAEL HYMANS

AMBERLEY

First published 2018

Amberley Publishing
The Hill, Stroud
Gloucestershire, GL5 4EP

www.amberley-books.com

British Library Cataloguing in Publication Data.
A catalogue record for this book is available from the British Library.

ISBN 978 1 4456 8233 4 (print)
ISBN 978 1 4456 8234 1 (ebook)

Typeset in 10.5pt on 13pt Sabon.
Origination by Amberley Publishing.
Printed in the UK.

Contents

Preface

After writing *Southern Region Through the 1950s* and *Southern Region Through the 1960s*, I presumed that would be the end of this short series. After the end of steam, I thought that there could be nothing of real interest to write about. But after doing a bit of initial research, I realised that the 1970s were interesting, but in a different way.

The authorities were having to cope with IRA bomb threats, bolshy unions holding lightning strikes and football fans who wrecked numerous trains. Bad winter weather continued to disrupt services, but even more so as steam engines coped much better than electric units that ground to a halt if ice formed on conductor rails.

There were far fewer enthusiasts standing on the end of station platforms or wandering round engine sheds, and as a result far fewer photographs were taken, so a big thank you to those that allowed me access to their photographic collections.

I enjoyed writing the book and hope you enjoy reading it just as much. Now, about those 1980s…!

Chapter 1

1970

£220 Million Plan

The Southern Region management presented a £220 million plan covering the next decade to the Minister of Transport. They wanted to spend £6 million more each year on improvements. They foresaw that enlargements to London termini would not be required. However, improvements to track and signalling and the introduction of modern stock would give 95 per cent punctuality in summer and 85 per cent in winter. They planned on replacing 200 carriages every year, each with a lifespan of twenty-five years, giving a fleet of 5,000 coaches. There would be three types of rolling stock: inner suburban high density with open-plan design with sliding doors; outer suburban based on the 4-VEPs but with sliding doors; and for express services on the Bournemouth line the existing design would be kept, but would need another forty coaches to cope with extra demand. Since electrification of this route, annual revenue had increased from £2.8 million to £4 million, which was £630,000 more than expected.

They also wanted to electrify all of their lines, which meant that 308 EMU coaches would be needed to replace their 342 DEMU coaches. This involved 230 route miles. On the Hastings line it would mean singling the track through all the tunnels due to its unique loading gauge.

They also foresaw the end of all loco-hauled services, apart from inter-regional trains.

Signalling was not forgotten and they envisaged replacing 555 signalboxes and 1,950 signalmen's jobs with thirteen new power boxes to cover the region.

A new station at Ludgate Circus was proposed and this would replace Blackfriars and Holborn Viaduct. Plans to rebuild Victoria would depend on proposed Heathrow and Channel Tunnel schemes. London Bridge would be totally rebuilt.

Passengers would benefit from a change in ticketing, whereby they could go to any London terminus rather than having a specific one printed on their tickets.

A total of 440 of the Region's larger stations would be modernised, with another 130 smaller stations having their buildings replaced with modern structures.

Resignalling

Wimbledon took over traffic control from Woking on 25 January, and two weeks later control was also passed from Southampton to Wimbledon.

Full colour light signalling and track circuit block working was introduced between Petersfield and Havant on 11 January. This meant that signal boxes at Rowlands Castle, Idsworth Crossing and Buriton Sidings were closed.

Surbiton panel box opened on 1 March, controlling the main line from Berrylands to West Byfleet and the branch lines from Surbiton to Effingham Junction and Hampton Court and from Weybridge to Chertsey. This meant the old boxes at Surbiton, Hampton Court Junction and Esher closed. The boxes at Hampton Court and Cook's Crossing were reduced to gate boxes.

Three weeks later the second stage of the conversion from semaphore signals took place. This was from Walton to Byfleet and the triangular junction at Addlestone and Chertsey. Six boxes were closed – Walton, Oatlands, Weybridge, Byfleet Junction, West Byfleet and Addlestone Junction. Addlestone and Chertsey boxes had to stay open to operate level crossings.

1 March saw colour light signals introduced between Weymouth and Bincombe Tunnel, meaning that the Upwey and Broadwey boxes closed.

Freight from Kent

Associated Portland Cement Manufacturers (APCM) had been building a new cement works at Northfleet since the late 1960s. This was on the existing site of Bevan's Works at Northfleet and replaced smaller plants at Cliffe Works on the Hoo Peninsula, Holborough Works at Medway, Johnson's Works at Greenhithe, Kent Works at Stone, and Metropolitan and Wouldham Works in Essex.

Six new kilns were brought into use. A new connection had to be laid from the North Kent main line to the site and this opened in April, with No. 6572 bringing one of the first loads of gypsum from Tonbridge via Hither Green. More chalk was also brought by train from Mountfield in Sussex and Theale in Berkshire. The new track formed a continuous loop around the site to negate the need for reversing. Coal was brought from Welbeck Colliery in Nottinghamshire.

There were also sidings to the south of the station. Class 33s were used as motive power to and from the site, but this necessitated them being fitted with slow speed control equipment. As Mountfield is on the Hastings line, some of the slimmer Class 33/2s had to be adapted with this equipment too.

Richborough Power Station was kept fed with coal from the Tilmanstone, Betteshanger and Snowdown Collieries.

Bad Weather

The start of the year began badly due to the weather, with snow and ice causing many delays and cancellations. 6 January became known as Southern's blackest day. A brief shower of freezing rain early in the morning in the Haywards Heath area caused a build-up of ice on conductor rails up to an inch thick, meaning no trains could run for up to five hours.

The 05.58 Brighton–Victoria was the first to be affected, but luckily this was being followed by the 05.10 Eastbourne–Bricklayers Arms locomotive-hauled van train which was able to assist it from the rear. The 06.46 Brighton–London Bridge became stuck fast at Balcombe. The following train, the 06.58 Brighton–London Bridge, tried to assist from the rear, but failed to move it. Diesel assistance was required, but these were becoming scarcer with the reduction in freight traffic and it was after 11.00 before a Class 33 arrived from Three Bridges to pull both stricken trains to Three Bridges. Northwards from there was not affected and the trains continued with the 06.46 still with a diesel on the front. The next train up was the 07.05 Brighton–Victoria, which also got stuck at Balcombe, but this was assisted from the rear by a loco from Haywards Heath. There was a train stuck at every signal behind these but they were gradually cleared by reversing them back down the line to Brighton, with many commuters giving up the struggle to get to work.

The closure of the line through Uckfield exacerbated the delays, with the only alternative route from Brighton and Worthing to London being via the Mid-Sussex line.

The Eastern Division was also hit, although not as badly, but there were no trains between Tonbridge and Orpington or from Maidstone East.

To try to combat criticism of their recent troubles, the Southern produced a four-page pamphlet that was given to passengers, detailing just how freezing rain affected the services and how they were trying to develop an oil that could be sprayed onto tracks that would prevent ice forming and was resistant to being washed away by rain.

Industrial Action

Strikes were not uncommon at the time and Waterloo was hit by a lightning one on 13 May when porters, shunters and ticket collectors walked out. This meant that loco-hauled services could not enter the station as they could not be uncoupled. These services were terminated at Clapham Junction or even Basingstoke. The BBC put out a broadcast asking passengers to help by closing their doors after alighting, and this proved to be quite successful.

More trains had to be cancelled when lightning strikes occurred at Waterloo on 11 June between 12.00 and 15.00, and again on 19 June when no trains ran for 24 hours. Passengers crammed onto the few trains that did run. They were not amused by adverts on the sides of London buses at the time declaring that 'British Rail is travelling'.

Regulars on the Waterloo line also suffered delays on 4 June due to a fire on Lambeth Road Bridge just outside the terminus. All power had to be turned off to allow the fire brigade access to fight the fire.

Industrial unrest, caused by rest day working grievances, spread to Farnham and Guildford on 13 July. The strike lasted 24 hours with no advance warning being given to passengers.

Accidents

On 9 January an eight-car train derailed when leaving the sidings at Plumstead with the leading coach of No. 5033 tilting over, blocking the Up line. The breakdown crane arrived from Hither Green, hauled by E6033, and normal service resumed by 15.30.

On the evening of 11 February, Class 47 No. 1872 became derailed leaving Millbrook freightliner depot. It was re-railed the following morning.

Six days later at about 16.00 a 4-EPB, No. 5254, at the rear of a ten-car train derailed at Borough Market Junction. It was formed of ECS, so no passengers were hurt, but the rear of the unit was left hanging over the bridge crossing Cathedral Street. This caused major disruption, with many complaints being made about a lack of information, the incident even being mentioned in Parliament. It was said that there was no time or place where an accident could have caused more disruption.

On 18 April a ballast train from Three Bridges double-headed by Nos 6566 and 6570 was passing Purley when three hoppers jumped the track, causing considerable damage not only to the track but to signalling equipment and the station platform. It took 24 hours to repair the damage.

On one of the rare occasions that one of the unreliable Class 74s was working, E6109 collided with a stationary 2-EPB at Chertsey station, damaging the loco

The rear carriage of Hastings DEMU No. 1034, which hit a lineside hut after derailing near Godstone on 10 June 1970. (Courtesy Peter Beyer)

2-HAP No. 6167, the rear unit of the 07.41 from Hove, derailed as it entered London Bridge on 16 November 1970. (Courtesy Peter Beyer)

and derailing three wagons. Following this accident on 1 June, the whole class was withdrawn temporarily to have their brake block slack adjusters checked at Eastleigh Works, but all were back in service three days later. E6109 was sent to Crewe Works for repairs to be carried out.

Due to a derailment at Hildenborough on 10 June, the 13.43 Hastings–Charing Cross had to be diverted via Redhill. This train became derailed east of Godstone with the eighth and twelfth carriages jumping the track. The last one made contact with a concrete lineside hut, causing considerable damage. This hut probably saved the unit, No. 1034, from falling down an embankment. The front unit, No. 1005, was unaffected and was able to continue.

On 15 July, 4-BEP No. 7015, while being used as a parcels train, struck a lorry carrying 7 tons of stone on a crossing at Chartham. The driver of the lorry and the guard on the train were both killed.

On 16 November, the 07.41 from Hove derailed as it entered London Bridge. The last coach of the train, 2-HAP No. 6167, derailed and the rear bogie ran up the platform ramp, causing it to tilt over 45 degrees. There were no injuries.

Unusual Workings

Specials from Gatwick on 17 and 18 March left for Leicester. They were double-headed trains with Class 25s Nos 5219 and 5222 on the 17th, and 5216 and 5222 on the 18th.

A Western Region Blue Pullman operated an enthusiasts' special on a return trip from Surbiton to Carmarthen on 25 April.

A ten-car train made up of GWR DMUs (two three-car units and one four-car unit) formed a mystery excursion from Paddington to Seaford. From there it continued to Hastings.

A Class 35 Hymek was in charge of the 17.23 Portsmouth Harbour–Cardiff on 25 April.

From 16 to 20 March, driver training between Stewarts Lane and Tonbridge was undertaken by an MLV (Motor Luggage Van) hauling eight SPVs (Spot Fish Van).

Closures

Freight facilities were withdrawn from Robertsbridge's private sidings on 1 January and from Branksome, Farnham and Wareham in May.

The yard and wharf at Littlehampton closed on 4 May, as did yards at Southampton Town Quay, Gillingham (Kent), Brockley Lane, Battersea Wharf, Horsham and Salfords. A week later Eastbourne, Haywards Heath and Worthing lost their freight services. Littlehampton closed on 18 May, and Cosham, Fareham and Woking closed at the start of June. Freight facilities were withdrawn from Stewarts Lane in November.

At a TUCC (Transport Users Consultative Committee) enquiry into the closure of the Mid-Hants line, Aldershot & District Traction Co. Ltd, who were supposed to be operating the substitute bus service, were questioned as to how they were planning to do this as they were so short of drivers that they were cancelling existing services.

The Hastings to Ashford via Rye line received a stay of execution when the Traffic Commissioners refused to grant licences for improved bus services until some road improvements had been made. These would not be done in the foreseeable future.

Miscellanea

Chalk falls at Folkestone were the source of delays, so sensitive wires were installed alongside the track and these rang alarms in signal boxes and turned lights to red should falls occur.

Delays are caused on the railways by a variety of reasons, and on 18 February vandals threw a metal bar onto the track between Winchester Junction and Wallers Ash Junction. Unfortunately, it bridged the conductor rail and the running rail, causing a short circuit. It also burned the running rail so badly that the engineer had to take possession of the track, causing longer delays.

Other delays were caused by staff. On Saturday 7 February the driver was sitting at Platform 6 at Orpington station on the 08.00 to Victoria, waiting for a green light. After fifteen minutes he realised that he was sitting at the head of an empty train. Although the service left from Platform 6 Mondays to Friday, on Saturdays it left from Platform 1!

Another train that suffered delays due to crew problems was the 20.18 Charing Cross–Dartford service on 23 April. Their train was held up because there was a LMR freight train in front and two crews – one LMR and one SR – were arguing who should take the train forward. Eventually the freight train was reversed into a siding and both crews were sent home.

Some 2-BIL and 2-HAL units were converted for parcels work, meaning loco-hauled parcel trains would only be needed at peak periods. They were re-classified as 2-PAN and numbered from 061 upwards.

Plumpton Racecourse was the venue for a pop concert over the spring bank holiday weekend. Many extra shuttle services were laid on from Haywards Heath and Lewes. Other scheduled services made an extra stop there. The festival did not attract as many festival-goers as hoped by the organisers. It was still busy though as I found out on the Tuesday morning while commuting to London when the 06.47 from Eastbourne was 'invaded' by hippies carrying tents, backpacks, guitars and so on. Being only eighteen at the time I found it quite amusing, but judging by the looks on the faces of the other commuters I was in a minority.

Two private excursions ran from Victoria to Glynde for the opera house, one using 5-BEL unit 3052 and the other using Southampton boat-train stock hauled by E6039.

On 6 September, four preserved engines left their temporary home in the old Pullman car sheds at Brighton, bound for their new home at Tyseley. These were No. 30777 *Sir Lamiel*, No. 30925 *Cheltenham*, LSWR T9 No. 120 and L&YR No. 1008. Their place was soon taken up by more locos – Nos 44027, 49395, 63601 and 4771 *Green Arrow*. These had come from Leicester via Stewarts Lane.

Although there were many excursions to the Southern from WR and LMR stations, there were fewer trips in the other direction. However, one such trip was run from East Croydon to Bristol using Hastings six-car units Nos 1033/5. Due to hardly any advertising the trip was very poorly patronised.

On 17/18 January, a new bridge was rolled into place between Virginia Water and Chertsey, taking the M3 over the line.

Tomato traffic from the Channel Islands continued with two daily (except Mondays) trains – one to Washford Heath, Birmingham, and the other to Crewe. On Sundays they went to Manchester and Severn Tunnel Junction.

Brighton Works were demolished, leaving the signal box as the only railway building left standing on the east side of the line.

Brighton Belle unit No. 3051 was put back into service with only four cars following a fire at Brighton in September 1969.

Unit No. 7808, a 4-VEP, was the first unit to be delivered from York in the new blue/grey livery.

Bomb scares were not uncommon at the time. On 14 September a Victoria–Folkestone Harbour boat train was evacuated at Bromley South and delayed for forty minutes before it was confirmed as being a hoax. Earlier in the month two 4-CEP units, Nos 7123/70, on ECS caught fire between Sittingbourne and Faversham. The front two coaches of No. 7123 and rear two coaches of No. 7170 were damaged and there was speculation that it was caused by a bomb. The undamaged carriages were subsequently formed into one unit – No. 7170.

4 October saw the last locomotive-hauled Newhaven boat train. Multiple units took over, with the Down train being part of the 09.48 Victoria–Eastbourne, with four coaches being detached at Lewes. The return journey at 17.18 ran back to Victoria without coupling up to any other services.

There was an attempted bullion robbery on 27 November between London and Staplehurst when thieves broke into a train carrying the valuable cargo on its way to Italy. They started throwing out silver bars and boxes of money at intervals along the line. A ganger saw some of the items being thrown out and informed the authorities. A similar attempt had taken place in 1955, when thieves successfully replaced gold bars with lead on a train bound for Paris.

The Class 74 electro-diesels, converted from Class 71s, became the most unreliable class of locomotive on the entire rail network.

The 18.12 Waterloo–Portsmouth Harbour broke away between the seventh and eighth carriages when leaving Petersfield. While waiting for assistance the driver collapsed and died.

A new service to Portsmouth from Waterloo was due to start on 4 May using new 4-CIG/4-BIG units. It is a good thing the new service was not well advertised as none of the new stock was ready, leaving the 4-COR/4-BUF units to struggle on. And struggle they did because there was a heatwave at the time and many units were having problems, including running hot axle boxes. The inaugural trip finally ran on 2 June when 4-BIG No. 7049 and 4-CIG No. 7338 with the new official saloon, DB975025, on the rear formed the 08.50 from Waterloo. Regular services started the following week when No. 7339 joined the above units to make a twelve-car train.

The Swanage branch had no through trains so the service could easily be withdrawn when replacement bus services could take over. The service was run by a single Hampshire DEMU, which was stabled at Bournemouth overnight. The unit returned to Eastleigh after a week for servicing and another unit would take its place.

One train made it through from Waterloo though. This was on 25 May, spring bank holiday Monday, when a Ramblers' excursion was run made up of 12-TC hauled by an electro-diesel as far as Bournemouth, from where two Class 33/2s propelled the train to Swanage.

2-BIL No. 2036 was on a Littlehampton–Brighton service on 5 September 1970 when photographed at Worthing. A sister unit was going in the opposite direction. (Courtesy J. Aston)

Another 2-BIL, No. 2086, this time waiting to leave Waterloo on 24 April 1970.

Staying at Waterloo and a gleaming No. 74005 couples up to its train.

On 20 May 1970 a double-headed Class 33 train of tankers heads through Eastleigh. (Courtesy Ian Nolan)

3H unit No. 1102 is seen at Southampton with a Portsmouth and Southsea service in January 1970. (Courtesy Neil Instrall)

2-BIL No. 2096 enters Eastbourne on a Hastings–Brighton stopping service.

4-COR No. 3113 heads south through Clapham Junction towards Littlehampton on 22 May 1970. (Courtesy C. Nash)

2-EPB No. 5674, seen after arriving at Waterloo on 24 April 1970. (Courtesy C. Nash)

Class 73 E6035 in original BR blue livery on a van train at Chichester.

An unusual sight at Chichester was Warship D870 *Zulu*, seen returning to Bognor Regis with an excursion to Exeter St Davids. (Courtesy Trevor Tupper)

Staying with unusual sights in Chichester and Class 47 No. 1616 is seen with the Royal Train carrying Prince Phillip. (Courtesy Trevor Tupper)

D6558 and D6566 are seen at Salisbury while heading a West Sussex Railway Touring Trust excursion from Worthing to Ilfracombe and back on 30 August 1970.

Ruston & Hornsby Class 07 D2991 is seen at Southampton Docks. (Courtesy Ian Nolan)

3-TIS No. 486 032 waits at Ryde Pierhead on 4 August 1970. (Courtesy Ian Nolan)

At Ryde Esplanade 3-TIS No. 486 031 was captured on camera on 3 September 1970. (Courtesy S. Nash)

A sorry sight in August 1970 was a very overgrown Ventnor station. (Courtesy Ian Nolan)

Chapter 2

1971

Kent Freight

The Class 33s on the coal and cement trains to and from APCM at Northfleet were found to be underpowered and some were replaced by Class 45s and 47s from other Regions. This meant that up to seven 'foreign' locos could be seen daily, handling up to ninety block trains each week. There were twenty-one 1,200-ton coal trains, nine 550-ton gypsum trains and about sixty 800-ton cement trains

Richborough Power Station was being converted from coal to become an oil-burning power station. By the end of the year, block oil trains were running to Thames Haven/Coryton, changing locos at Hither Green.

Freightliner Services

From 4 January, an extra Freightliner service was introduced from Millbrook to Swansea. The train left for Swansea at 05.58, returning from Swansea at 13.40, and used the stock from the Liverpool/Manchester service that was idle at Millbrook at those times. A Class 47 was rostered to run the service but it was not unheard of for a South Wales Class 37 to be seen on it.

Closures

Cambria Junction Signal Box, near Brixton, was closed in February with its work being taken over by Loughborough Junction box. It was demolished about four weeks later.

In May freight facilities were withdrawn from Hastings, Faversham, Queenborough, Dartford and Strood. Staines lost its freight facilities on 31 August.

Brighton's Kemp Town branch, which had been kept open for freight use only, closed on 14 June. However, on 26 June it re-opened for the day to run special passenger services. These were the first passenger trains to run over the line for thirty-eight years. An hourly service ran from Brighton using 'Tadpole' unit No. 1205. The service ran from 10.00 to 21.00 and was extremely well patronised, with all profits going to the Woking Orphanage. Another attraction at Brighton on the day was No. 92220 *Evening Star*. It had been hauled from the Preston Park store and specially prepared for the event.

Catford Bridge and Lower Sydenham Signal Boxes were closed in April, as were the adjacent sidings and connection to Sydenham Gas Works, when colour light signals were introduced.

In August the DOE gave permission to close the Mid Hants line between Alton and Winchester. The exact closure date would depend on when replacement bus services could be introduced. Alton would then become a terminus.

Herne Bay Signal Box closed on 22 August. Chislet Colliery station closed on 4 October while Fareham West box closed on 5 December.

Industrial Action

Drivers started 'go slow' industrial action from 5 April, which had an impact on services, especially during the morning and evening rush hours. It ended on 13 April. This led to many cancellations, especially on the South Eastern Division, where fifteen to thirty rush hour trains were being cancelled daily.

On 16 June it was announced that there would be a planned reduction in services of about eighty trains each day until a shortage of staff could be resolved. The rail unions responded that these cancellations would mean a loss of earnings of about £3 per week for their members and announced a ban on rest day working. Management backed down and the announced cancellations would not go ahead. Irregular cancellations continued with 24 June being the worst day, with 131 trains being cancelled.

Accidents

On 22 January the 16.40 Margate–Victoria service was derailed near Brixton. Two carriages left the track but stayed upright. There were no injuries but it caused considerable delays.

At Sheerness on 26 February the 17.16 from Victoria, made up of five 2-HAP units, entered the station under clear signals but failed to stop in time. It cleared the sand drag and demolished the buffers. The leading coach, minus its bogie, slid across the concourse and demolished the booking hall and the station's outer wall. Regrettably, a lady in the booking office was killed. Thirteen other people, including the train crew, were injured. It was concluded at the enquiry that the driver had suffered some sort of blackout approaching the station and had collapsed over the controls, with his weight holding down the dead man's handle.

Eleven wagons on the Severn Tunnel Junction–Norwood Junction derailed between Codford and Wylye on 26 February. It took two days to clear the line and resume normal services.

On 4 April, access to Stewarts Lane depot was cut off due to engineering works. Warship Class diesel No. 826 *Jupiter* needed refuelling so was sent to Selhurst but derailed at Streatham station on its way there. Services were disrupted for six hours while it was re-railed.

On 28 June, the main London–Brighton line was blocked when the twelve-car 06.41 Norwood Junction–Brighton train derailed at Copyhold Junction, north of Haywards Heath, when the points moved under the leading carriage. The error was down to the signalman at Haywards Heath, who mistakenly thought that the train was held at the protecting signal on account of a point failure. However, the failure occurred after the train had passed the signal and had the effect of destroying the locking on the facing points, leaving them free to be moved under the train.

Both Down lines were blocked and with the breakdown crane on the Up through, only the Up local was available for use. Most Brighton trains were re-routed via Horsham and Littlehampton. Passengers for Eastbourne did not fare so well, having to use a bus between Three Bridges and Haywards Heath. The 09.48 Newhaven boat train was run using DEMU stock and ran to Uckfield, from where buses were laid on.

At Surbiton on 4 July a wagon on the 08.25 Clapham Yard–Farnham ballast train jumped the track. It was the twenty-fourth wagon of the forty-five-wagon train and derailed after becoming buffer locked with the wagon in front. One of the derailed wagons hit a point machine, destroying it, causing the facing points to change and throwing the wagons into the path of the passing 09.50 Waterloo–Portsmouth Harbour which was travelling at over 70 mph. 4-VEP No. 7714, the leading coach, derailed but stayed upright for over 580 feet before its bogie collided with a girder of a rail overbridge, throwing it onto its side. It slid for another 500 feet. The two coaches behind derailed but stayed upright. Luckily, there were no serious injuries. The ballast train was double-headed by E6025 and E6033, which sustained damage to one end. The accident occurred because the buffers on the unladen twenty-fourth wagon had risen over the laden twenty-third wagon while being marshalled at Clapham.

A derailed goods train came to rest up against a passing 4-VEP at Surbiton on 4 July 1971.

On 15 December the 09.15 Cardiff–Portsmouth Harbour, hauled by Class 35 No. 7037, passed a colour light signal at danger while entering Portsmouth & Southsea station and collided with the rear of the 11.02 Victoria–Portsmouth Harbour service standing at the platform, pushing it forward about 4 feet. Nine passengers and seven railway staff were injured but none seriously.

Unusual Workings

The Emperor of Japan arrived at Gatwick on 5 October and was taken to London in a five-coach train, including two Pullmans and a Royal Saloon. It was hauled by No. 821 *Greyhound*. Drivers from Stratford had unsuccessfully insisted on crewing the train as they argued they had the monopoly on all Royal trains in the South East, as they worked the Royal trains to the Derby. This probably accounted for the Class 42 being used rather than the customary Class 31 used on Royal trains.

No. 818 *Glory* operated a similar train on 7 December when the King of Afghanistan visited.

Christmas parcels services saw 2-PAN units Nos 061 and 063 pressed into service. Several windows had been smashed while stored at Oatlands Sidings and these had been boarded up with hardboard. 4-Sub No. 4115, still in green livery, was also used for Christmas mail workings.

On 22 May the 22.02 Victoria–Bognor Regis train was unusually run using a Class 73 hauling the usual 4-CEP/4-BEP stock. This was because the only driver available was not trained to drive EMUs.

The Royal Train to the Derby race meeting was operated by D5659 from the Eastern Region in spotless blue livery.

Miscellanea

Uckfield station was re-sited to the other side of the main road through the town so the level crossing could be permanently open to traffic as through services to Lewes had ended.

The newly introduced REP units had to be temporarily withdrawn so defects in the tyres of the motor bogies could be addressed.

The three 4-GRI units, Nos 3086–88, were withdrawn in November. They had been rebuilt in 1962 from 4-RES units made in 1937/8, which had been made for the Waterloo–Portsmouth and Bognor services. A goodbye railtour using Nos 3086/7 was run on 6 February from Brighton, visiting Seaford, London Bridge, Horsham, Littlehampton, Portsmouth Harbour, Guildford and Victoria before returning to Brighton.

No. 70000 *Britannia* had been stored at Redhill for about two years, but on the night of 14/15 March it was towed to Old Oak Common with its ultimate destination being the Severn Valley Railway.

The 8-VAB (VEP and Buffet) No. 8001 was only officially diagrammed to work on summer Saturdays, but it was often pressed into service up to three times a week on its old running of the 08.56 and 14.56 Bournemouth–Waterloo and 11.47 and 17.30 return services.

A new crossover was brought into use at Clapham Junction which allowed trains from the Brighton lines access into Waterloo.

West Country No. 34023 *Blackmore Vale* and an assortment of other rolling stock were hauled to Haywards Heath on 27 September by No. 6570, and would continue their journey to the Bluebell Railway by road.

The last 2-BIL and 2-HAL units were withdrawn in August, although four 2-BIL units were kept for a railtour in September. Three of these units, Nos 2111/35/40, ran an enthusiasts' special from Waterloo via Richmond, Broad Street, Watford Junction, Euston, Crystal Palace and London Bridge to Blackfriars. 4-COR units took over the Brighton–Portsmouth service from the withdrawn units.

The two double-decker units, Nos 4001/2, were taken out of service on 1 October. They were twenty-two years old and had covered over 700,000 miles on the route between Dartford and London. They had been introduced as an experiment to overcome overcrowding, but although the eight coaches could accommodate 1,100 passengers as opposed to 800 on a conventional suburban unit, they took too long at stations for passengers to board or alight and the experiment was not taken any further.

The new PEP units were introduced and started a long period of trials before entering revenue-earning service. These were three high-capacity units – two four-coach units painted in rail blue and a two-coach unit left in unpainted aluminium. Trials would last twelve months and 250,000 miles would be covered to evaluate the units before a decision would be made on future orders.

Transatlantic liners had been losing customers to aircraft but there was an increase in cruising. Many of these cruises left from Southampton on a Saturday or Sunday and ended on a Friday. Extra boat trains were run to cope with the demand. 3 December was typical, when seven boat trains ran from Southampton to Waterloo, with five returning the following day. Two weeks earlier though, ten trains ran – four in the Up direction and six Down put a strain on rolling stock availability.

The last Class 42 Warship diesels left Waterloo on 3 October with Nos 811, 812 and 823 being among the last of the class to put in an appearance there. Class 33s took over the running of their services to Exeter but they were limited to trains of eight coaches – nine if the heaters were not required. Class 42s were able to haul ten coaches. These shorter trains led to overcrowding. On the 17.05 departure on the first Friday of the new service it was reported that about eighty passengers were forced to stand.

The TOPS numbering system for locomotives was introduced with the first two digits being the class number and the next three being the number within the class. The first to be altered were Classes 76, 83 and 84.

The branch from Chichester to Lavant, which had not been used for several years, was brought back into use in October. A new industrial development was given planning permission, providing that the gravel was removed by rail. When in full production, a train was scheduled to leave every two hours during 08.00 and 18.00.

Trains of Volkswagen cars from Ramsgate increased from two to six every week and ran to Frome and Doncaster.

D817 *Foxhound*, still in maroon livery, enters Waterloo during October 1971. (Courtesy Stuart Ray)

Another Warship at Waterloo in October, this time in blue livery, was No. 812 *The Royal Naval Reserve 1859–1959.*

4-COR No. 3161 leaves Waterloo on a Reading via Richmond service during October 1971. (Courtesy Stuart Ray)

No. 4107, a 1942 design of 4-SUB, enters Waterloo during October 1971. (Courtesy Stuart Ray)

No. 4125, a later design of 4-SUB, is seen having worked a suburban train into the Windsor line platforms at Waterloo. (Courtesy Stuart Ray)

On a gloriously sunny October day, Class 74 E6109 reverses onto its train at Waterloo. (Courtesy Stuart Ray)

Lancing station had seen better days when photographed on 29 November 1971. Only the bare bones of a shelter remained and the loading bay behind the passengers was no longer in use.

4-COR No. 3133 passes Camberley Signal Box on 22 June 1971 with a Waterloo to Aldershot service. (Courtesy Kevin Lane)

Chapter 3

1972

Brighton Belle

The last day of service of this famous train was on 30 April after nearly forty years' service. All three units were used. Nos 3052 and 3053 worked the timetabled service until 19.00 at Victoria, whence No. 3053 worked the later services alone. No. 3051 worked a railtour that left Brighton at 12.20, running via Three Bridges, Littlehampton, Bognor Regis, Lewes, Newhaven Harbour and back to Brighton. It then formed the 18.50 'Cheese and Wine Special' to Victoria, where it coupled up to No. 3052 and worked the 22.30 'Champagne Special' back to Brighton. Tickets on this latter train cost £10 return and included a three-course meal and champagne. The return journey for the passengers was by a Special Buffet train leaving at 00.30. The Belle units were kept at Brighton and were still available for private charters.

One of the more famous regulars on the Brighton Belle was Sir Laurence Olivier. His patronage of the train became well known when it was proposed to withdraw kippers from the menu. Although he was successful in keeping the kippers, he was less successful in saving the train.

To commemorate the withdrawal of the Brighton Belle, the RCTS organised a railtour from London that made its way to Portsmouth and then along the South Coast, visiting Bognor and Littlehampton before traversing the Mid-Sussex line to Three Bridges, then south to Eastbourne and Hastings, returning via Newhaven to Brighton for a non-stop run back to Victoria. The original tour planned for 8 April sold out very quickly, so an identical tour was arranged for the week before. No. 3053 was used on both days. The regular Belle service had to use 4-COR No. 3130 coupled with No. 3051, as No. 3052 was unavailable.

There were reports that an American wished to purchase all the units and export them to the States where they would become a tourist attraction. British Railways said they would sell the units to the highest bidder, irrespective of nationality.

Allied Breweries Ltd purchased three second class Pullman parlour cars for £22,500 and three motor brake cars, Nos 291–293, for £14,500.

Another motor brake, No. 289, was sold to the landlord of the Little Mill Inn at Rowarth, Cheshire, and was turned into a restaurant named The Derbyshire Belle. It was restored to original Pullman livery and gained a cocktail bar with a kitchen built into the guard's section. It was unloaded onto track laid behind the inn.

Golden Arrow

The Golden Arrow ran for the last time on 30 September. It was hauled by Class 71 E5013 leading a van, five coaches and four Pullmans. The loco carried both French and British flags above the name board. A train continued to run on Golden Arrow timings using EMU stock and connected with a Calais ferry at Folkestone Harbour.

Five of the Pullmans were put up for sale, with offers being invited to the BRB Technical Centre at Derby. The vehicles in question were Parlour Cars Nos 301 *Perseus*, 302 *Phoenix*, 308 *Cygnus* and Kitchen Cars Nos 306 *Orion* and 307 *Carina*.

Through Services

The 08.27 Southampton–Birmingham New Street and the 16.29 Poole–Birmingham were both extended to Liverpool Lime Street. A Sunday service linking the two cities was also introduced. The Poole–York train was extended to Newcastle.

On the downside, services to Cardiff from Portsmouth via Bristol were reduced to one daily trip in each direction.

The Brighton–Exeter service was run from May on Saturdays only and was in the hands of Hastings units. Two units were needed to cope with the summer demand but only one unit was used from October.

Industrial Action

The South Western division suffered industrial action from 31 January, when drivers started a 'go slow'. Over 100 trains were cancelled most days, with suburban services bearing the brunt. Normal working resumed on 14 February.

Long-suffering passengers had more disruption to cope with when the miners' strike started to have an effect on the railways. Initially heaters were turned off to conserve power, but these measures were not nearly enough, and 40 to 50 per cent of off-peak trains had to be cancelled. Voltage reductions also caused failures to signals and automatic barriers. Diesel services were not affected.

The strike brought some unusual workings for the Hastings units as well, one of which was the 14.05 Victoria–Folkestone on 18 February. The Down journey was uneventful but the train had difficulty climbing back up the 1 in 37 bank from the harbour and had to be assisted by a diesel shunter.

Reduced services on many lines meant crews were not able to earn as many bonuses and drivers at Littlehampton vented their annoyance by walking out on 22 March, giving the travelling public no notice of this action.

On the Central Division, drivers played what they called 'The Periscope Game'. This derived from the times when guard's vans were fitted with periscopes but the practice of fitting these had stopped with later trains. The drivers were refusing to drive trains without a periscope fitted unless a second man was provided in the cab. If this train was cancelled and the following train also had no periscope the driver from the first cancelled train was instructed to be the second man in the following train. He would then refuse to do this if that train did not have a seat fitted for a second man. 4-SUBs were lacking in both and EPB or VEP units were substituted for these in some cases. Drivers were also abandoning their trains on running lines in stations rather than taking them to sidings, causing trains to be re-routed around the obstruction. In one case all running lines at Dorking were blocked by abandoned trains and one train to Bognor finally reached its destination three hours late. This unofficial action was mainly confined to drivers at London termini and gained little sympathy from crews in outlying areas.

The 'go slow' and overtime ban were made official on 17 April. The timetable was thrown into complete disarray, with up to 130 trains being cancelled daily and hardly any trains running after 20.00. The unions called off the strike from 24 April after a ruling from the Industrial Relations Court, but the drivers at Waterloo were not happy and staged an unofficial strike that day, returning to work the following day.

Accidents

On 8 January a serious collision took place at Horsham when a ballast train, double-headed by E6027 and E6010, ran past a red signal and hit the rear of the

The aftermath of the accident at Horsham on 8 January 1972 between a 4-BEP and Class 73 E6027. (Courtesy Peter Beyer)

12.02 Victoria–Portsmouth Harbour via Bognor Regis. E6027 was very badly damaged but the crew survived as they had taken refuge in the rear cab. The rear of the passenger train 4-BEP was also very badly damaged. Seventeen passengers were injured. Several bogie bolster wagons were derailed, with some overturning and damaging the supports of a road overbridge, closing it to road traffic. The accident occurred over a misunderstanding of the coupling of the train to its wagons. After E6027 coupled up to E6010, the driver reported having difficulty starting both diesel engines from his cab. The second man started uncoupling the air brake pipes between the two locomotives, having first closed the cocks on both. He was then told that this would have no effect, so he reconnected the pipes but failed to re-open the cocks. He managed to start both locos and the driver, using diesel power, started towards Three Bridges station, where he was to switch to electric power. He had not realised that the brakes on the second loco and the first four wagons were not working until he tried braking for a distant signal at caution. He realised this was not working and so tried braking again, unsuccessfully, before making an emergency application. The train ran the signal, through a junction and into the Down platform where a Portsmouth train was standing, pushing it

Class 47 No. 1630 was extensively damaged after derailing at high speed at Eltham Well Hall on 11 June 1972.

forward about 200 feet. The guard and the driver were blamed for not carrying out a brake test before it was too late. E6027 was badly damaged and was written off.

A serious accident occurred at Eltham Well Hall on 11 June when an excursion hauled by Class 47 No. 1630 from Margate to Kentish Town derailed. The train was running late and failed to slow for a speed restriction of 20 mph in place for a right-hand bend. The guard had tried to alert the driver of his speed by two short brake applications but these were ignored. The speed of the train was estimated at 65 mph. The driver and five passengers were killed and 129 were injured. Blood tests subsequently found that the driver had over three times the alcohol level allowed for motorists. He had been drinking while at Margate before starting his duty and even had alcohol in the cab. He was found to be solely responsible for the accident.

The 18.45 Acton–Wimbledon goods train hauled by E6001 passed a red signal on the approach to Wimbledon station on 12 October and collided with the rear of the stationary 19.05 Holborn Viaduct–West Croydon 4-EPB, No. 5220, pushing it forward 35 yards. The rear of the EMU was badly damaged. Seven wagons were derailed. Eleven passengers were injured, but none seriously. The driver, who had been trapped in his cab, was found solely to blame for the accident, and it was somewhat surprising as he had worked that same train for the three previous nights. There were reports that his breath smelled of alcohol but this could not be tested as there was no equipment available to do so, even though it had been recommended by the report into the earlier accident at Eltham.

On 7 September the 14.05 from Chessington South to Waterloo derailed after leaving Clapham Junction. The four-coach train left the station on a red signal and derailed on the facing crossover when the points moved beneath the train. Two coaches derailed but the train stayed upright. Four passengers were slightly injured.

A passenger opened a carriage door on the wrong side at Kent House on 6 November and was struck by a passing Sheerness train on the fast line. It was ripped from its hinges and landed on the live rail, causing a short circuit. Five passengers were injured.

On 16 December two trains collided at Copyhold Junction where four tracks converge into two. The 21.28 stopping Brighton–London service formed of 4-VEP units Nos 7768 and 7771 was hit by the 21.45 non-stop Brighton–London made up of CIG/BIG units Nos 7366, 7045 and 7363. In all fourteen coaches were derailed, with many overturning. The junctions of both Up and Down lines were destroyed. The all-steel carriages stood up well to the impact, with only a few passengers sustaining injuries, but it took over three days to clear the lines. Even then the point work was not replaced, meaning the slow lines were out of action, leading to delays and cancellations. It was near the end of January before the new track could be manufactured and replaced.

Unusual Workings

The Class 42 Warships that had been displaced from their duties at Waterloo were subsequently to be found on road stone trains from Westbury to Merstham and Gatwick. This was in connection with the building of the M23 and M25 motorways.

Class 52 Westerns were also used on these trains. Timekeeping for these trains was not good, and together with breakdowns they often affected passenger train timings in the area. On 20 June a train headed by No. 825 *Intrepid* bound for Gatwick derailed at Dorking Town. This was near the site of a derailment two years earlier and it ripped up the newly laid track from that incident.

On 19 and 20 April, two 4-COR units, Nos 3132 and 3159, were loco-hauled as no motorman could be found to drive the electric units.

Class 31 No. 5688 was on Royal duties on two occasions – the first on the train to Tattenham Corner for the Derby on 7 June and again on 13 June, when it met the Grand Duke of Luxembourg at Gatwick Airport and took him to Victoria.

In June a Royal Train just consisted of a 4-BEP, No. 7019, for a journey from Waterloo to Portsmouth Harbour. The following month a 4TC was hauled by E6008 for a trip from Windsor & Eton (Riverside) to Portsmouth, but the original destination of Southampton Western Docks had to be abandoned due to a dock strike.

The Royal Train was used again on 26 October when a Class 31 left Waterloo at 23.10, stopping overnight at Andover, before continuing in the morning to Gillingham in Dorset.

Another class of power was provided for the Royal Train when a Class 52 hauled the train from Southampton to Barry.

On 20 January No. 4771 *Green Arrow* was hauled dead from Preston Park, Brighton, on its way to Norwich. LNER 04 2-8-0 No. 63601, which had been kept at Selhurst, was hauled away to Wigston on 7 August.

LMR 0-6-0 No. 44027 and 0-8-0 No. 49395 were hauled from storage at Preston Park bound for Leicester on 18 June. Other steam locos being towed were 9F 2-10-0 No. 92203 and Standard 4MT 4-6-0 No. 75027, which left Liss with other preserved rolling stock on 24 October behind Class 47 No. 1726 on their way to Eastleigh.

The Hastings units had been used for excursions on Saturdays, but these units were then regularly being used on the Brighton–Exeter service. This latter service was supposed to be for the summer only but proved so popular that they were kept on for the winter. Demand for excursions was so high that it was worth bringing in loco-hauled stock to run these. Two of these hauled by Class 33s from Eastbourne were a mystery tour to Chesterfield and to Westbury for Longleat.

In July the shipping service to the Channel Islands ran into problems both with fog engulfing the English Channel for several days and *Sarnia* having mechanical problems. The *Invicta* was brought from Dover to substitute and on 21 July the *Maid of Orleans* left Jersey on the overnight service but had to dock at Newhaven because it was needed for cross-Channel services. Two trains were waiting to greet the vessel at Newhaven – one to take passengers to London and the other to take passengers back to Weymouth.

An MLV, No. 68010, arrived at Eastbourne under its own power on 24 September, where it was attached to the rear of the 15.28 to Ore. It returned, heading the train, before returning to Victoria on the rear of the 18.03. Two more MLVs worked together on a newspaper special from Victoria to Bognor. It had to go via Lewes because of engineering works on the Mid-Sussex and Brighton lines.

A single Class 45 was used on a Brent–Northfleet coal train (weighing 1,800 tons). As a rule Class 4 diesels had to be double-headed as their slow acceleration had knock-on effects on passenger trains behind them.

The Gatwick Airport–Ripple Lane aviation fuel train had been seen in the hands of Class 47s and, less often, Class 37s.

Closures

The Swanage branch closed on New Year's Day. The line stayed open as far as Furzebrook Sidings (between Worgret Junction and Corfe Castle) for freight traffic. The last day of passenger services saw two Hampshire DEMUs, Nos 1110 and 1124, operating the service between Wareham and Swanage. The last train was additional to the advertised timetable and was the 21.45 from Wareham to Swanage, returning at 22.15 through to Bournemouth. Both these trains carried a headboard reading 'The Purbeck Flyer'. An excursion, The Purbeck Piper, formed of Hastings DEMUs left Blackfriars and also ran over the line.

This was the last day of working on the Swanage branch and 3H No. 1110 prepares to leave Wareham with a train full of enthusiasts.

The following day, No. 1110 was sent to Tunbridge Wells West for use on the Oxted line. On 4 February a ballast train made it to Swanage to pick up permanent way huts.

At Lewes, rationalisation of the layout saw Lewes 'A' and 'D' boxes being closed with 'B' being the only box left. As a result, it was simply renamed 'Lewes'.

Crawley lost its freight facilities on 19 June.

Weymouth Town's freight facilities were withdrawn on 14 August. Full-load freight facilities were withdrawn from Margate, Ramsgate and Folkestone East during December.

Platforms 20 to 22 at London Bridge were closed permanently.

Miscellanea

From 3 January, 4-CORs had no regular workings out of Waterloo after their last route, Waterloo to Reading, was taken over by CIG units. However, failures of these latter units meant that the odd 4-COR still put in an appearance.

Colour light signals were introduced on the Chessington line between Motspur Park and Chessington South on 30 January. A new ground frame was introduced at Tolworth for movements to and from the coal depot. Tolworth Box closed on 29 January and Chessington South a day later. Moreton Gate box was closed on 16 February with the installation of lifting barriers.

The 8-VAB unit was painted in blue/grey livery.

Two new sidings were opened in February. The first was between Dean and Salisbury for the English China Clay workings and the second on the other side of Salisbury at Quidington.

Freight services from the Channel Islands were withdrawn from Weymouth on 28 February and transferred to Southampton on a temporary basis before being moved to Portsmouth. All freight from the Channel Islands went to Portsmouth from October. The freight was handled by two vessels, the *Jersey Fisher* and the *Guernsey Fisher*.

Southampton Maritime Freightliner Terminal opened on 10 April with two trains booked to arrive and leave – one to/from Ripple Lane, Birmingham, and the other to Trafford Park, Manchester.

Crews were trained to drive Class 31 diesels as these were to replace the Class 35s that were being withdrawn.

Epsom Downs terminus station, which once boasted nine platforms, was reduced to having only two – the former Platforms 4 and 5. Apart from a scissors crossover just outside the station, all point work was removed and the stock that used to be stabled there overnight was stabled elsewhere.

A man ran amok at London Bridge station on 17 June, attacking staff and property. When police arrived he managed to jump on a departing train and evaded arrest. He alighted at Orpington and carried on with his wrecking spree, breaking station and carriage windows while attacking more staff. He then threw a metal bench onto the track, which shorted out the electrical circuits. He ran along the track to Petts

Wood where he committed similar offences. He set off towards Chislehurst but was eventually stopped by police with dogs before he could wreak any more havoc.

4-CORs were all withdrawn from service by 1 October. Their last haunts were lines in East Sussex, being used on the Brighton–Hastings and Ore and Haywards Heath–Seaford stopping services.

A farewell tour was organised using Nos 3102/43 from Waterloo to London Bridge, Margate, Folkestone, Tonbridge and Portsmouth Harbour, returning via Horsham to Victoria. No. 3102 had been working the previous day – the last day of regular service – with a morning trip from Seaford to Haywards Heath before returning to Brighton. Nos 3136 and 3145 operated a relief from Brighton to Portsmouth and No. 3142 was scheduled for preservation.

The 1970s was the era of the football hooligan and on 16 September a group of around 100 supporters rushed the barrier at Victoria, overpowering the staff and boarding the 18.00 non-stop to Brighton. They then destroyed units 4-BIG No. 7048 and 4-CIG No. 7312, smashing light bulbs, lampshades, wash basins, pedestals, roller towels and cabinets as well as ripping down curtains. Passengers were assaulted and beer cans were thrown at buffet car attendants.

Motorail services were introduced on 26 May between Dover and Stirling. The northbound services left on Saturdays and Sundays, with the return services running on Fridays and Saturdays. The inaugural service consisted of three coaches and three carflats hauled by Class 33 No. 6577. At Kensington it combined with the Kensington–Stirling train. The Class 33 then pulled the combined train to Willesden Junction, where the loco was changed.

A high-density 4-PEP unit, No. 4001, had been undergoing trials for a number of months and entered service on the South Western Division in August. After a couple of months it was transferred to the Central Division and then to the Eastern Division.

A new promotional campaign was launched to try to increase patronage on the Portsmouth–Brighton–Hastings line. It was marketed as the 'Coastway' service and as part of the launch a 'Miss Coastway' beauty competition was held at a hotel in Brighton.

A new Sealink Terminal was opened at Folkestone with roll-on roll-off facilities for vehicles. It was part of a £9 million investment programme that included the purchase of two 5,000-ton multi-purpose ferries. The new facilities meant that the transfer between ship and boat was completely under cover.

The Southern had to buy another 130 new luggage trolleys. Of the 135 purchased two years previously at a cost of £2,000, there were only five left. One even turned up as far away as Paris!

Another 3H, No. 1130, was seen at Fratton during 1972 with a Southampton–Portsmouth working.

The Brighton Belle in corporate blue livery at Brighton on 6 April 1972.

Occasionally the Belle would be hired out for enthusiasts' trips and here No. 3053 is seen on one such at Eastbourne.

A stranger to the region, D1061 *Western Envoy* was seen resting at Fareham. (Courtesy Trevor Tupper)

A view of Charing Cross as it was in 1972 with both rail blue and blue/grey units to be seen. (Courtesy Stuart Ray)

Class 74 E6104 took part in the open day at Old Oak Common in September 1972. (Courtesy Neil Instrall)

Chapter 4

1973

London Termini

At Holborn Viaduct the short Platforms 2 and 3 were removed and the ground was levelled. Platforms 4 and 5 were renumbered 2 and 3 from May. Track was lifted on the line to Farringdon via the tunnel under Holborn Viaduct and the island platform that was Ludgate Hill station was levelled, leaving little sign of the former station.

It was intended that the original 1864 LCDR lattice girder bridge at Blackfriars would eventually be demolished, leaving only the easternmost iron-arch structure to carry the remaining tracks across the river. The Curator of Relics at the British Railways Board put in a claim for one of the three massive cast-iron LCDR crests that adorned the bridge. He also requested the facing stones from one plinth. These plinths were built from some of the stones of the old Westminster Bridge, which was demolished in 1861. It was also agreed that some of the more unusual inscribed destinations in the stonework of Blackfriars station frontage would be incorporated in the rebuilt Blackfriars station.

Renewal of Grants

At the start of the year, the Minister for Transport Industries announced that he was renewing all grant aided subsidies for a further year. Lines that benefitted from these subsidies were: Bournemouth–Weymouth (£655,000); Brighton–Ore and branches (£1,062,000); Brighton–Portsmouth (£1,230,000); Southampton–Salisbury/Fareham–Eastleigh (£907,000); Reading–Basingstoke–Salisbury (£147,000); and Reading–Redhill–Tonbridge (£610,000).

Channel Tunnel

A Green Paper was published outlining the studies in hand and laying out arrangements under which the tunnel would be built and operated. It was estimated that the twin-bore rail tunnel would cost £366 million without interest. British Railways recommended a route that started from a passenger terminal at White City, where connections to the rest of the country could be made. The line to Clapham Junction would be enlarged and electrified. Two new running lines would then follow the existing route to Balham. It would then enter a new tunnel, exiting near South Croydon where it would run parallel to the Oxted line as far as Woldingham, from where a new line would be built to join the existing Redhill–Tonbridge line between Godstone and Edenbridge. From there the line would be widened and reconstructed as far as Pluckley, and a new line would be constructed from there to the tunnel portal.

A White Paper was published on 12 September stating that it would be in the national interest for the tunnel to be built. It would consist of two main tunnels, each carrying a single line, both connected to a single service tunnel. It stressed that for the tunnel to reach its full potential the problem of the loading gauge on the Southern Region would have to be addressed, and to this end a new line from the tunnel to London would have to be built. Agreement on financing had been agreed with the French government and the international group responsible for its construction. Through traffic would be supplemented by a shuttle service carrying vehicles from a terminal at Cheriton and one at Fréthun, just outside Calais. On 17 November the two governments signed parallel agreements with British and French Channel Tunnel companies setting out arrangements for the financing and construction of the tunnel.

11 miles of track between Ashford and Appledore were to be singled and work was to be carried out on bridges and level crossings so that Channel Tunnel car-carrying vehicles, which were outside the loading gauge, could be tested there. Permission had already been given for withdrawal of passenger traffic on the Ashford–Hastings line, although local councils were considering subsidising the service. Nuclear waste from Dungeness left by rail so the line from Appledore to Ashford would have to stay open.

The TGWU opposed the building of the tunnel as it believed that it would take jobs away from its members, who worked at ports in Kent. It also felt that if a fire broke out in the tunnel it would become a '32-mile coffin'. The British Channel Tunnel Co. Ltd defended the fire risk by pointing out that each car-carrying wagon would be designed to contain any fire within the wagon. Passenger trains could be stopped within one minute with all passengers being led to safety in an adjoining tunnel, which could be sealed off. They would then be rescued by a train in the other running tunnel.

Industrial Action

The new year did not bring an improvement in industrial relations. In February and March, the drivers' union ASLEF staged a number of one-day strikes and a period of non-co-operation. Drivers refused to operate 4-SUB and 4-EPB units so management rostered CIG, BIG and VEP units to cover these duties, thus keeping some sort of suburban service running. This had the knock-on effect of leaving main line services short of stock, and passengers had to endure much overcrowding. Services using REP and TC formations could not be split and were largely unaffected. Football specials and excursions were all cancelled. A number of diesels from other Regions were also 'failed' with minor defects by Southern drivers with at least ten engines – mainly

Class 47s – being stranded at various depots, but Class 31 No. 5687 was also spotted stranded at Guildford and Class 35 No. 7044 was seen at Fratton.

On the Central Division some drivers refused to go at more than 40 mph, playing havoc with timetables. Other drivers found 'faults' with their train and refused to take them from the sidings, while others refused to drive trains that had no working speedometers. On the South Eastern Division drivers again refused to take out trains without speedometers unless there was a second man in the cab. An end came to the dispute on 16 March.

October saw the next strikes, when drivers at Victoria and Streatham Hill refused to work any main line electric units because the cabs were draughty. They did not get any support from drivers at other depots, but on 19 November crews from Waterloo, other London depots and Basingstoke staged another 24-hour walkout.

The strikes weren't confined to the railways and on 7 November Sealink ferries to the Isle of Wight were cancelled when crews withdrew their labour.

Accidents

On 14 March, the 06.20 from Margate collided with some ECS while approaching Victoria. The front bogie of 2-HAP No. 6025 was derailed. No one was injured but 700 commuters had to walk along the tracks to the station.

On 30 May, a parcels train made up of 4-SUB units Nos 4691 and 4376 became derailed when approaching Waterloo, blocking the Up and Down fast mains, the Up main relief and the Down Windsor slow lines. The 12.30 Waterloo–Weymouth was

4-SUB No. 4635 collided with a bridge parapet at Horsham on 12 July 1973. (Courtesy Peter Beyer)

trapped in Platform 11 and had to be cancelled. Also stuck at signals was the Up 11.22 from Guildford. Passengers had to be detrained and walk back to Vauxhall.

At Sidcup on 2 June, an Acton–Strood freight train derailed. Ten hoppers loaded with coal blocked the Up and Down main lines and the Down passenger loop, causing much disruption for two days before the lines could be re-opened.

On 25 June at Cannon Street at 09.00 a 12-CEP train from Ramsgate passed signals at red and hit the side of a 10-EPB train. There were no injuries, but the station had to close until late in the afternoon.

On 12 July 4-SUB No. 4635 passed two ground signals at danger when leaving the sidings at Horsham. The unit was derailed by a set of catch points and collided with a bridge parapet, which crushed the cab, killing the driver.

August and September were not good months for derailments on the Brighton line. A freight train derailed on the Quarry line between Merstham and Redhill tunnels, which necessitated the relaying of 2 miles of track. On 11 September, between the tunnel and station at Balcombe, another freight train derailed despite a 10 mph temporary speed restriction over the re-laid track. On 26 September, a third freight train jumped the rails at Balcombe on track that had also just been re-laid. A temporary restriction on short-wheelbase vehicles was imposed.

The Isle of Wight did not escape the year without accidents and on 10 September two units, Nos 035 and 045, were damaged while being shunted. The couplings within the units held but the couplings between the units gave way, damaging both cabs.

On 3 September 1973 at Dorking, No. 4745 ran into the back of No. 4661, which was so badly damaged it was withdrawn. There was no official investigation into the accident. (Courtesy Peter Beyer)

Unusual Workings

The Duke of Edinburgh travelled by train from Sheffield to Leatherhead on 16 February. His train consisted of five vehicles pulled by Class 25s Nos 5218 and 5219.

On duty for the Royal Train to the Derby on 6 June was Class 31 No. 5690, from Old Oak Common. The four-coach train was made up of the Royal Saloon and a BR maroon restaurant car with a blue/grey BSK (Corridor Brake Second) at either end.

Her Majesty was not so lucky on 20 July when she visited the Naval Dockyards at Portsmouth as 4-BEP No. 7019 was used, albeit in ex-works condition.

A 'League Liner' was a twelve-coach, totally first-class train introduced for exclusive use by the Football League to take fans to matches. The train was equipped with a 'Kick Off Disco' – a cinema coach with four televisions showing video-taped programmes and two coaches equipped with headphones giving passengers the choice of three music channels. The League then chartered it to clubs, who set their own fares and provided their own catering. It was hired by Charlton Athletic Football Club on 29 August for their supporters, whose team was playing at Brighton. Unusually, E5005 pulled the train for the whole journey, which had started at Dartford, even though it needed running round at Bricklayers Arms and Hove. On the homeward journey the driver forgot to stop at Charlton to let the fans off (was he a Brighton supporter?!) but stopped at Woolwich Arsenal just in time for fans to catch the last train home.

Visiting Class 47s were fairly common, being the main source of motive power on excursions from other Regions. They also worked stone trains and oil trains from Gatwick. Less common were Class 37s, but Nos 6733 and 6831 were seen at Salfords.

A Class 31 had a regular working on Southern metals, working a Bristol–Portsmouth parcels train. Class 52s were also regular visitors on stone trains from Merehead Quarry.

Another Class 31, No. 5809, was on Royal duties when used to take the President of Zaire from Gatwick to Victoria. No. 5809 was joined by No. 5690 when they pulled four Royal Train vehicles, taking the Duke of Edinburgh to Eastbourne on 26 November. They left the next day for Plymouth via Kensington.

Closures

The last day of the Mid-Hants Line was Sunday 4 February. The previous day the two-car units had proved insufficient to carry the number of enthusiasts wishing to travel, so on the Sunday three-car units were added. No. 1121 worked with No. 1125, while No. 1122 worked with No. 1130. The last trains were the 20.40 Southampton–Alton with the return trip being at 22.08. Between Ropley and Alresford it had paint thrown at it and one 'bomb' hit a passenger looking out of a window.

Brighton MPD lost its allocation of locomotives when the last shunters were transferred. Shunting duties at Brighton and Newhaven were supplied with locomotives from Selhurst. Walford Road coal depot in South London, formerly owned by the LMS, closed on 30 April.

Miscellanea

Two Golden Arrow Pullmans, Nos 302 *Phoenix* and 307 *Carina*, left Brighton on 8 January for destinations on the SNCF, travelling via Dover and Dunkirk. The following day two more left for Gateshead. One found its way to Ashford while No. 281 stayed at Brighton.

Trials took place using Class 33s on the Weymouth Tramway on 15 February, pulling boat trains. These were successful, although the service by then had been reduced to only one train a day. This meant that the only passenger service in the country booked to be hauled by a Class 03 had come to an end.

On 9 March the Isle of Wight ferry MV *Shanklin* collided with the pier head at Ryde in thick fog. Extensive damage was caused to the pier, but luckily not to the railway. Several cars were stranded there though and had to wait until they could be craned onto the car ferry *Fishbourne*. The pier was mended by October. A new car ferry, *Caedmon*, went into service on the Portsmouth–Fishbourne route in July.

The Freightliner terminal at Southampton became fully operational and ran services to Ripple Lane, Leeds, Birmingham, Manchester, Glasgow, Liverpool and Carlisle.

Excursions from outside the Region to Hastings were re-routed via Ashford and Rye. Class 47s were not allowed over this line, so many excursions had to be double-headed by Class 33s. One excursion from Cleethorpes arrived behind No. 6586 and E6038.

Some lines in the Region only continued because they were grant-aided. One of these was the Reading–Tonbridge line. To try to encourage more use of the line, 150,000 households were sent discount travel vouchers along with timetables and fare tables. Motorists were encouraged to park at stations and continue their journeys by train. The unreliability of units did not help the line's cause though. For instance, on 26 May Oxted unit No. 1308 failed at Wokingham on its way to Tonbridge. It was rescued after an hour by a similar unit, No. 1313, on the following service, the 10.25 from Reading. This unit failed at Chilworth and both units had to wait another hour until the next service, Tadpole unit No. 1205, which managed to push them both as far as Redhill. It continued alone to Tonbridge and started its return journey, the 13.46, albeit about forty-five minutes late. This unit then disgraced itself by breaking down between Leigh and Penshurst. A loco from Tonbridge helped it into Redhill where it combined with the following service to continue to Reading.

Another publicity campaign was carried out in Hampshire. The Portsmouth–Salisbury and Fareham–Eastleigh shuttle services had been called 'Hantsway'. Again, timetables and places of interest and events to visit were delivered to hundreds of households, together with six vouchers worth 10p each for use on Awaydays. The lines were in receipt of a £1 million subsidy and it was hoped that increased usage would decrease the need for this subsidy. The fact that some services on these lines had been cut in May had not been good for public relations. Even worse was that when complaints were received from the public about the lack of toilet facilities on the DEMUs, with only one coach having a toilet and no connection between coaches, especially on those that went through to Bristol, they were told they were suburban rather than inter-city services, and if they required toilet facilities they should travel via London! Another suggestion by a BR press officer was that passengers should 'nip out smartly at each stop'. Patronage did increase though and Western Region DMUs were brought in to ease overcrowding.

4-VEPs entered service on the Eastern Division from 7 May. These were Nos 7842–7851 and worked on London–Kent Coast semi-fast services. Also from that date changes were made to inter-Region freight services and Western Region crews were allowed to work through on Southern metals. Crews were trained on the routes using a single-car DMU from Old Oak Common on 29 April and on a three-car DMU from Paddington and Southall during the early part of May. Some freight services leaving the region, including the Hoo Junction to Thame oil train that used to change engines at Old Oak Common, now worked the whole journey using Southern crews.

The first 4-PEP entered revenue-earning service on 4 June. No. 4001 worked a trip for the national press before working between Waterloo and Hampton Court. The other unit was delivered shortly afterwards and the two ran trouble free until 20 July, when No. 4001 failed on the 08.26 Waterloo–Hampton Court. Later that day, No. 4002 became defective on the 13.34 trip from Waterloo, and the following week 2-PEP No. 2001 replaced No. 4001 on services. From August all units were coupled to form a ten-coach train and worked an intensive diagram from Charing Cross and Cannon Street to Dartford, Bromley and Sevenoaks. Publicity for the new train and a market research team were on board the train. Several stations had to have their platforms raised to accommodate it. Trials were to continue for a further two years until 250,000 miles had been run. It failed at Eltham Well Hall with brake trouble early in the morning of 23 August, causing disruption to rush hour traffic to Charing Cross, Holborn Viaduct and Cannon Street. It returned to the South West Division and services from Waterloo on 17 December.

The first fully air-conditioned train on the region ran on 21 June. It was a private charter to Messrs Olivetti. The stock was the latest Mark IIF vehicles manufactured at Derby Works. The train was made up of four LM and four ER FOs (First Open), two SR RBs (Restaurant Buffet) and a Mk II BSO (Brake Second Open). The empty stock was worked from Clapham Yard to Waterloo early in the afternoon to allow the restaurant car staff to stock up. It was hauled in by Class 33 No. 6514, but was hauled out by Class 47 No. 1571.

New station buildings were opened at Dartford in June, meaning that the old buildings on Platforms 1 and 2 could be demolished. A new Platform 1 was brought into use with a connection to Platform 2 at the London end, which meant that the station then had four running lines through it.

An exhibition was staged at Brighton on 30 June in aid of Woking Homes and Nos 34051 Sir *Winston Churchill*, 33001, 30587, 45000 and LSWR No. 245 were all pulled from storage at Lovers Walk to be displayed in the station. They were joined by electric shunter DS75, as well as No. 6566, E6012 and instruction unit No. 053.

The Seaford branch from Newhaven Harbour was singled in July and was worked tokenless block over the former Up line.

From 1 October, when VEPs ousted EPBs on suburban services to Guildford via Cobham, first-class seats were re-introduced after a gap of thirty-two years.

Six new Motorail services were announced during the year throughout the network, with three starting from the Southern. These were Brockenhurst–Stirling, Dover–Newton Abbot and Dover–St Austell.

Another 203 sets of points were fitted with remote controlled electric point heaters. Of these, eighty-four replaced life-expired gas heaters. This brought the total number of point heaters on the Southern Region to 735.

Class 33s that were operating over the tramway to Weymouth Harbour were fitted with a flashing light and a bell. These were only fitted while the loco was working over the line. During the autumn, there was much disruption to the timetable due to trains skidding on wet leaves, which created flat spots on their tyres. To alleviate the problem, an experimental train was run that squirted water from pairs of nozzles suspended 1 foot above the track. Between these were wire brushes in contact with the track. The train, which doubled as a de-icing unit in the winter, travelled at 10 mph when operational. The train ran three times every day in November between Faversham and Dover.

There was an unusual sight at Strood on 19 September, when a Class 73 in charge of seven 100-ton oil wagons stalled on a sharp bend leading up to Rochester Bridge. The following train, formed of a 4-CEP and 2-HAP, was used to push the train up the gradient. There were a lot of flashes and bangs and much smoke from electrical motors but it managed to push the stricken train to the summit before it carried on, apparently none the worse for its exertions.

Planning permission was sought to redevelop Brighton station. If approved, the listed building would be demolished and a new building with a fourteen-storey office block would be erected over the new station. The Brighton Society rigorously objected to the proposals.

On 24 November the carriage sheds at Effingham Junction were badly damaged by fire. Several units stored inside were also damaged, including 4-VEP No. 7852, which was barely seven months old. Other units damaged were Nos 4299, 4381/5, 4640/71, 5130 and 7820. Two of the 4-SUBS were written off while No. 7820 swapped carriages with some from No. 7852, which was damaged in an accident with No. 4607 at Durnsford Road depot in December.

2H No. 1119, introduced in 1957, is seen at Hastings on a service to Ashford during 1973.

3D unit No. 1312, introduced in 1962, passes through Clapham Junction on a Victoria–East Grinstead service. (Courtesy Neil Instrall)

Class 08 No. 3809, introduced in 1953, is seen on duty at Clapham Junction. (Courtesy Neil Instrall)

2 HAP No. 6036 waits at Strood before setting off on a service to Maidstone West. (Courtesy Stuart Ray)

Class 33 No. 6513 heads through Clapham Junction during August 1973. (Courtesy Neil Instrall)

This 2-HAP, No. 6076, was photographed at Margate during September 1973. The black triangle was there to warn waiting Post Office staff that there was no guard's van at the other end of the unit. (Courtesy Neil Instrall)

Class 33 No. 6549 is seen at Waterloo with a semi-fast to Exeter St Davids during April 1973. (Courtesy N. Instrall)

The 'Z' on the head code identifies this unidentified Class 47 as being on a railtour as it heads through Chichester in July 1973. (Courtesy Trevor Tupper)

Class 33 No. 6523 was photographed at Exeter St Davids in September 1973 before heading towards Waterloo. (Courtesy Neil Instrall)

One of the unreliable Class 74s, E6103, is seen at Clapham Junction during August 1973. (Courtesy Neil Instrall)

A view of 4-TC and 4-CIG cabs at Waterloo during April 1973. (Courtesy Neil Instrall)

A battered Class 33 at Eastleigh Works in May 1973. (Courtesy Trevor Tupper)

Chapter 5

1974

London Termini

Work was continuing on Blackfriars station. This was the first major work undertaken by the new British Railways Property Board in conjunction with King's College, which owned part of the site. The work, which would take another three years to finish, would provide 100,000 square feet of office space on seven floors over a new concourse. The LT station beneath was also being updated. The BR station was accessed by rail over four bridges; three of these were to be rebuilt, including the main one over Queen Victoria Street, and the fourth one was to be demolished. The new station would keep three terminal platforms and two through roads to Holborn Viaduct. One of the problems with the renovations was that beneath the station was one of the largest cold stores in the country. There were fourteen separate chambers under the station and twenty-one more on land owned by King's College. After eighty years of freezing, ice had formed 20 feet below ground level. Defrosting this too quickly could have endangered the buildings above it so caution was required. Hot ammonia gas was pumped through pipes, and when the ice started to melt it was knocked off and carried outside. It was left to melt in a pit and the water was then pumped into the Thames.

The rebuilding of London Bridge station was approved by the Ministry of Transport. The £5.4 million scheme would reconstruct the passenger concourse, ticket hall and electronic train indicators as well as improving access to the Underground. Many of the facilities on the station were temporary structures still in place after bombing during the Second World War. A canopy was also to be erected on the forecourt to allow passengers arriving at the station by bus to stay under cover. A new footbridge was erected, connecting the two sides of the station. The rail approaches to the station would also be revised and re-signalled, with the six tracks used by the Central Division being reduced to four, with the old Brighton Down fast and slow lines being taken over by Eastern Division services. This meant the closure of Cannon Street from 3 August to 9 September, with some services terminating there being cancelled and others being diverted to Victoria, London Bridge, Charing Cross, Blackfriars and Holborn Viaduct. By October there were numerous complaints that points were failing at least once every day, causing delays for many commuters. Complaints were also being made that if trains left their starting points late, time would be made up by not stopping at intermediate stations. This led to much overcrowding on following stopping trains.

Feltham Signal Box

A new £6 million signal box opened at Feltham on 8 September, and this replaced forty-five older boxes. The new box controlled 351 colour light signals and 112 points, covering 70 miles of track encompassing Richmond, Bracknell, Frimley and Norbiton, taking in the branches to Windsor and Shepperton. This opening also meant the total demise of semaphore signalling on the South West Division. It was one of thirteen new boxes that would eventually control the whole of the Southern Region.

The new box required twenty-one signalmen, including seven men to disseminate information, five regulators and one cleaner on duty. These replaced the 155 men needed in the old boxes. There had been a shortage of signalmen in the area, which often led to the cancellation of some services. The box also covered fifteen public level crossings, eleven of which were monitored by CCTV. One, Sunningdale, remained manned, and three were automatic.

Industrial Action

The year did not start well due to industrial disputes. On 10 January drivers who refused to work normally were sent home. Other members of staff responded to this by walking out themselves. However, the following day the policy of non-co-operation was lifted and there was a marked improvement in services. Staff from Slade Green still refused to drive EPB units not equipped with speedometers and refused to work on Sundays, and an overtime ban continued. This action meant there were many idle staff on Sundays, so management decided to halve the number of these idle station staff and guards. This led to further walkouts by guards from Selhurst on 28 January and Brighton on 29 January.

7 February saw more disruption when a freight train driver at Hither Green refused to take his train to the Eastern Region, which was on strike. He was sent home, which led to drivers at Victoria, Stewarts Lane, Grove Park, Orpington, Addiscombe, Gillingham and Faversham walking out in support of him.

Signalmen also staged unofficial action in November. A walkout on 4 November by men on the Eastern Division caused widespread disruption with passengers arriving at ports on boat trains having to be taken all the way to London by bus. Signalmen on the Western Division also walked out on 17 December, bringing a halt to all services on the Bournemouth line west of Basingstoke, and Portsmouth–Salisbury and Fareham–Eastleigh diesel services.

Accidents

Another freight train derailed south of Balcombe Tunnel on the main Brighton line, and was the third such derailment on the section of line in six months. The derailed freight train was the 02.20 from Norwood Junction headed by No. 73108.

The derailed wagons blocked both lines as well as severing telephone lines, causing the closure of the line for three days. Trains to Brighton were re-routed via the Mid-Sussex line and Littlehampton or by diesel power to Uckfield, where buses took the travelling public to Lewes. At one time there were 4,000 passengers waiting at Haywards Heath for a bus. How they must have rued the short-sightedness of closing the link between Uckfield and Lewes.

4-EPB No. 5323 ran away without passengers or crew from Caterham station on 30 March before operating the 06.49 to London Bridge. A downhill gradient helped the unit to speeds of up to 25 mph. It ran through Purley and South Croydon to East Croydon, where staff tried unsuccessfully to jump aboard. It was switched into a siding at Norwood Junction, where it hit the buffer stops, sustaining only minor damage. It had run for over 9 miles. A full report was ordered by the Department of the Environment.

At Dorchester on 24 August a railwaymen's special returning from Weymouth to Hereford headed by No. 47236 ran through a red signal and over a set of catch points, sending it right through the sand drag and off the end of the track. Six passengers, members of the Hereford Staff & Social Club, needed hospital treatment and twelve more were treated on site. The rear ten coaches were passed fit to continue their journey, departing at 23.45. It was several days, however, before cranes from Eastleigh and Bath were able to get the loco back on the rails.

A Class 33, No. 33058, collided with a 4-SUB, No. 4715, at New Cross Gate on 29 August. The SUB was badly damaged, with two coaches telescoping.

Eighteen stone wagons were derailed at Cuxton on 2 December, blocking the Snodland–Strood line and damaging Cuxton platform.

Unusual Workings

On 13 July, a 4-VEP unit was rostered to work the 05.10 Coulsdon North–Victoria instead of the usual suburban unit. This was because the week previously a murder suspect was reported to have caught the train and police wanted to walk through the train interviewing passengers.

On 17 May there was an unusual sight at Fareham when No. 46012 arrived with a stone train from Westbury.

Another unusual sight was at Portsmouth Harbour on 26 June, when No. 37064 worked an excursion from the Eastern Region.

Two more Class 37s were spotted double-heading an oil train through East Croydon on 3 April. No. 31013 was used for crew training in March to the Salfords oil depot.

On 9 August DEMU No. 1316 failed at Dorking Town while operating the 06.09 Reading–Tonbridge service. The following train was a Class 33 hauling a 3R unit. This was used to propel the failed unit, and thus led to the unusual sight of a Class 33 propelling one unit while hauling another.

No. 31295 was on Royal duties again when it took the King and Queen of Malaysia from Gatwick to Victoria.

Drivers at Redhill were given training on Class 47s, which meant they could work through with stone trains from Westbury to Ardingly.

No. 35028 *Clan Line* made a trial run in steam between Ashford and Tonbridge on 24 February. Then, on 27 April, it ran light from Ashford to Basingstoke via Redhill, Guildford and Woking, from where it worked the Merchant Navy Preservation Society's charter train to Westbury. At Salisbury it was detached and shunted into a bay platform, where it was replenished with water using a hosepipe from the gent's toilet! After returning its train to Basingstoke, it returned light to Eastleigh to take part in the open day. The charter train returned to Waterloo. It ventured further afield on 26 October, when it ran light from Ashford to Didcot before working specials to Stratford-on-Avon, returning in the evening.

Class 73s were used on some Channel Island boat trains over the quay at Weymouth during July.

The Central Division witnessed an unusually long train on 21 October, but this was not intentional. The loco-hauled 07.19 East Grinstead–London Bridge failed at Upper Warlingham. The following train, the 07.15 from Uckfield, made up of three DEMUs, assisted from the rear, and the seventeen-coach train made it into East Croydon. The failed train was hauled away and the train from Uckfield continued, albeit an hour late.

Closures

On 31 July, the Minister of Transport, Fred Mulley, stated that the Hastings–Ashford and Wimbledon–West Croydon lines would not close. He said they should be covered by the first obligation to operate a passenger network, which he would be imposing under Clause 3 of the Railway Bill. The Hastings–Ashford line was added to the list of Southern lines eligible for grant aids. These grants for the Region totalled £14,017,000.

The Minister confirmed his statement made in Parliament in a letter to the Southern Region, which concluded that closing the line between Wimbledon and West Croydon would have a detrimental impact socially and environmentally could not be justified.

Miscellanea

On 19 January, Anthony Crosland told the House of Commons that the plans for the Channel Tunnel were officially abandoned, but said the plans would be kept in case the project was revived.

The annual open day in aid of Woking Homes was held at Brighton, with the locos still kept at Lovers Walk, Preston Park, being hauled into the station. None were in steam and most had coupling rods removed. Apart from these attractions, DEMU No. 1115 ran a shuttle service to the sheds at Lovers Walk, where enthusiasts could go down into one of the pits and walk under a unit. Demonstrations were given on how the steam crane could lift a carriage. The lower goods yard could be visited by riding in an open second coach pulled by No. 09017. Over £1,000 was raised.

Forty-two 2-HAP units were due to be downgraded to second class only. They were Nos 6001–6021 and 6024–44. The two intervening numbers were not converted because they had been fitted with experimental automatic couplers and were being used on tests on the Eastern Division. Conversion involved screwing up the armrests, removing the carpets and obliterating the first class logos. They were renumbered 5901–42 and re-classified 2-SAPs. The work had been completed by May.

A new timetable was introduced on 6 May, but due to a shortage of guards and drivers, 115 trains of the 4,086 due to run daily had to be cancelled. Further services were cut if staff phoned in sick. An intensive recruitment campaign was run, which brought the number of cancellations down to fifty-one by October. Some services had improved though; for example, there was an hourly service from London to Brighton that ran all night. Patronage on these trains was disappointing, however, and from October, when the winter service was introduced, this was reduced to two hourly trains at 00.25, 02.25 and 04.25, with the intervening service only going as far as Gatwick. The Waterloo–Weymouth service was also supposed to enjoy an hourly service during the day, with trains leaving at thirty minutes past the hour between 06.30 and 21.30 and using the new stock. Some of the 4-VEPs and TC units were late being delivered, however, so stock had to be borrowed from other Divisions to augment the service. This was a twelve-car CIG-BIG-CIG formation made up of Nos 7377, 7053 and 7378. This formation worked until October, when it was replaced by the 8-VAB working with a 4-VEP.

The Eastern Division was not forgotten, with the times from Victoria to Dover Marine sped up from two hours to one hour forty-seven minutes.

Services within Hampshire were suffering from a shortage of stock and this was not helped when unit No. 1106 collided with No. 33117 at Eastleigh depot on 1 April. From July, the Western Region came to the assistance of the Southern Region by supplying DMUs to bolster stock on the Hantsway Bristol–Portsmouth Harbour services.

Reading station had alterations made to it to make it easier for Southern trains to use. A new platform, 4B, was built by widening Platform 4A and extending the embankment towards the station car park. The new bay platform would be electrified and would be long enough to take eight-coach trains. The work meant that Southern trains could enter the station without interfering with the Western main line.

The renumbering of locomotives under the TOPS scheme gained pace, with No. 33202 being be the first Hastings gauge Class 33 to be so treated. The last of the class to be re-numbered was No. 6508, which became No. 33008 in April.

Cracks had been found in several bogies of the new PEP unit, No. 4001, and the unit was sent to Eastleigh for repairs in late February.

In order for some high-speed brake tests to be made between Woking and Basingstoke using a REP unit, No. 3009, speeds of up to 115 mph were authorised.

Newly converted carriages were delivered from York to convert 3TCs to 4TCs to bolster capacity. These meant that Nos 301–3 were re-numbered 429–32.

Betteshanger Colliery was to be equipped for rapid loading of merry-go-round trains as part of the NCB's plan to add seventeen more collieries to the twenty-three already so equipped. This would be the first Kent coal field to be altered and was set to be operational by 1977.

Wimbledon East EMU maintenance depot was officially opened on 3 October by the Chairman of the British Rail (Southern) Board.

In November, heavy rain affected services across the region, but the area around Lewes was the worst affected, causing the line to Eastbourne to be closed for three days between 22 and 24 November as water covered the tracks at Glynde and Folkington. On 22 November, the 03.27 Victoria–Eastbourne paper train got through as the Class 73 in charge of it switched to diesel power. Buses were laid on until DEMUs could be organised to run a shuttle service. No. 33045 was summoned to work a 16.05 East Croydon–Eastbourne train, returning at 18.03 to Haywards Heath and back to Eastbourne at 19.50. Flooding in the tunnel at Lewes became worse and it had to be shut for diesel traffic as well. The following day it was cleared for diesels to operate again and a 6S Hastings unit, No. 1001, was brought in together with 3Ds Nos 1106/15/6/8 and 3H No. 1318. Electric power was restored on Monday morning. Another line to be affected was the Redhill–Godstone line, when flooding occurred in Bletchingly Tunnel with passengers having to be taken by bus.

Leaves on the line caused their annual havoc. To try to alleviate this, two de-icing units were converted to water cannon in an attempt to blast the offending leaves from the rails. Their efforts did not stop many SUB and EPB units having to be taken out of service with severe flat wheels, which resulted in many services having to be made up of shorter than usual trains.

The Transfesa depot opened at Paddock Wood on 28 October. Three trains arrived daily with fruit and vegetables bound for the New Covent Garden Market at Nine Elms.

Much of the Christmas mail traffic had been lost to roads but 4-SUBs Nos 4706/25 and EPB No. 5207 were used for seasonal deliveries. The only loco-hauled mail trains ran between Reading, Redhill and Tonbridge.

On 26 November Mr Anthony Crosland, the Secretary of State for the Environment, stated in Parliament that there was no way the government should approve or finance an investment of the magnitude of the high-speed rail link from London to the Channel Tunnel portal at Cheriton. He said that the cost had risen from £120 million in February 1973 to £373 million in May 1974. He went on to say that an upgrade of the existing tracks would be investigated, with 25 kV overhead wires being installed and the loading gauge altered to allow Berne gauge vehicles.

The number of freight train derailments led to a reduction in speed for coal or mineral wagons from 45 mph to 35 mph, which led to delays in passenger traffic following these trains. In November a number of fitted mineral trains were run with a specially equipped test coach that had dispensation to run at 45 mph.

By November the stone trains supplying material for the M23/M25 had ceased and the unloading facilities at Merstham were removed.

On Sunday 23 November a water main burst outside Waterloo station and badly flooded the Waterloo & City line, causing it to close for many weeks. 30 million gallons entered the tunnel, completely filling them at their lowest level, and pumping the water out took several days. All the stock was at the Waterloo end of the line and all the stock was flooded to above their wheel bearings and had to be removed to Wimbledon for examination. Signalling and other electrical equipment was also damaged.

At Paddock Wood on 3 December, a Dover-bound train had to be stopped because a man had been spotted riding on the outside. The youth ran away when the train stopped, explaining that he had no money for a ticket!

No. 022, ex-2-HAL No. 2669, was in departmental use as a stores unit when seen at Eastleigh on 13 August 1974. (Courtesy Arnie Furniss)

6L No. 1015 at Hastings during August after arriving from London.

Class 71 No. 71011 stands at Tonbridge on an unknown date in 1974. (Courtesy J Woolley)

At Redhill one day in August, Tadpole unit 3R No. 1204 was working a service to Reading. (Courtesy Neil Instrall)

Shunting at Eastleigh on 13 August 1974 was No. 07011, formerly D2995. (Courtesy Arnie Furniss)

The tramway on Weymouth Quay was a favourite with photographers. The sight of a full-length train making its way past parked cars is, sadly, no more. Here No. 33111 is in charge of a train to Waterloo. (Courtesy James Winnen)

Another view of the previous train on the quay. Note the bell above the buffer beam. (Courtesy James Winnen)

From one seaside resort to another and 4-CIG No. 7326 was at Platform 1 at Eastbourne prior to leaving for Victoria in August 1974. (Courtesy Neil Instrall)

Staying in Eastbourne, two 4-VEPs – Nos 7762 and 7851 – were also seen. The central road has since been removed. Note the lantern roof in the background, which was a feature of other LBSCR stations, including Lewes. (Courtesy Neil Instrall)

Missing a carriage, 4-VEP No. 7822 runs into Clapham Junction during July on a Waterloo–Portsmouth & Southsea service. (Courtesy Neil Instrall)

4-CIG No. 7398 was one of the second batch to be delivered between 1970 and 1972. They were later reclassified as 421/4 and renumbered 1801–91. At Waterloo in July 1974, the trolleys on an adjacent platform testify that the railways were still used for the transportation of mail for the Post Office.

Shunting at Tonbridge was Class 08 No. 08833. This was the most abundant of classes of diesels, with 996 being produced between 1952 and 1962. (Courtesy J. Woolley)

The Class 09s were very similar to the 08s, with the only difference being in their gearing, meaning they had a higher top speed at the expense of tractive effort. They were all allocated to the Southern Region and No. 09013 is seen here working at Dover. (Courtesy J. Woolley)

No. 71011, formerly E5011, was seen at Tonbridge in 1974. The class of twenty-four had been introduced in 1958–60 to handle freight and express passenger services in Kent. Ten were rebuilt as Class 74s. This example was withdrawn in in November 1977. (Courtesy J. Woolley)

No. 73142 was the last of the Class 73s to be introduced, and it was initially numbered E6049. In May 2009 it was renumbered again to No. 73201 and named *Broadlands*. It is seen here at Clapham Junction. (Courtesy Neil Instrall)

The Night Ferry stock is marshalled at Victoria behind No. 73129 on 13 April 1979. (Courtesy Kevin Lake)

Chapter 6

1975

London Terminii

The platforms at London Bridge were re-numbered 1 to 16; 1 to 6 were the High Level through platforms serving the South Eastern Division and 7 to 16 were the terminal Central Division platforms. The new signal box simply named 'London Bridge' took over the Central Division lines on 20 July. This meant that the old boxes at New Cross Gate and Bricklayers Arms closed. The old London Bridge box remained opened to serve the South Eastern Division and was renamed London Bridge (Eastern).

When fully operational the new box would cover 148 track miles (47 route miles). 5 miles of track on the South Eastern would be signalled for reversible running, with it being used for Up trains in the morning rush and Down trains in the evening. Of the eleven tracks approaching the terminus, seven were for South Eastern Division trains. This was an increase of two at the expense of the Central Division. This was said to be because the demand for services on the Central Division had fallen.

Charing Cross and Waterloo East stations had to be closed over the weekend of 1/2 November to allow the umbrella bridge in the forecourt to be removed. Signalling work was also being undertaken at London Bridge, meaning that services were diverted to Charing Cross.

Industrial Action

The new year did not bring any improvements in industrial relations. Signalmen who were members of the unrecognised union, the Union of Railway Signalmen, staged an unofficial strike on 6 February. Services west of Basingstoke were badly hit, with no trains running between Basingstoke and Weymouth or Fareham and Eastleigh. A week later the action escalated, with most services from Waterloo being hit. On the Central Division there were no services north of East Croydon and a series of shuttle services were run between towns to the south. The South Eastern Division was affected, but not as badly, with only the lines between Tonbridge and Redhill and Strood and Paddock Wood having no service.

Workshop Supervisors went on strike during late March and early April, but their dispute did not have a significant effect on services, except in that some trains had shortened formations.

Unofficial strikes hit Fratton depot on 5 May and Eastleigh on 17 May when drivers walked out over 'manning agreements'.

Guards suddenly withdrew their labour at Strawberry Hill on 30 June and a week later services to Waterloo were disrupted for a couple of hours due to a signalmen's dispute.

Yet another walkout occurred on 13 September. Drivers at Waterloo walked out as the management had refused to order a taxi for a driver whose train arrived at the station the previous evening so late that he had missed his last train home! The walkout caused wide disruption to suburban and main line services.

Accidents

An unusual accident occurred on 21 February at Woldingham, on the Uckfield line. A stolen car that was being chased by police crashed through a fence and down a steep embankment before colliding with the passing 18.09 from Victoria. The train was made up of three units, Nos 1319, 1123 and 1303. The accident caused the

The breakdown crane had to be summoned from Brighton to re-rail the brake van that had derailed while being shunted in Eastbourne yard on 20 May 1975.

train to divide between the first and second units. No. 1319 sustained some serious damage. No passengers were hurt and the car driver, a fifteen-year-old boy, was thrown from the car before the impact and was not badly hurt. He was lucky because the car lodged under the buffers and was pushed for quarter of a mile.

Another accident with a car occurred at Mount Pleasant Crossing, Southampton, on 31 March, when it crashed through the barriers and collided with the 19.30 Weymouth–Waterloo.

On 25 March yet another freight train derailed south of Balcombe Tunnel. Two loaded coal wagons on the 11.01 Norwood Yard–Eastbourne pulled by No. 73108 left the rails, blocking both Up and Down lines. Bus companies came to the rescue again until 17.30 when single line working commenced using the Up line. Both lines were back in use by the following morning.

It's not often that a loco gets involved in two derailments on the same day but this happened to No. 73128 at Eastbourne on 20 May. First, while shunting at 02.10 it became derailed at a set of spring points, blocking the goods yard. The 01.50 freight on its way to Eastbourne from Norwood had to be hastily diverted to Brighton. No. 73128 was re-railed using jacks. Found to be undamaged, it was allowed to continue its duties. Later in the day, a rake of vans it was propelling became badly

Class 33 No. 33041, having been embedded into the front of 4-SUB No. 4704, is seen at Bricklayers Arms Junction on 11 September 1975.

The damage to the cab of No. 4704 could clearly be seen after the two trains had been separated.

derailed, trapping the loco in the yard. The crane had to be called from Brighton to re-rail the wagons and release the loco.

A serious accident occurred near Bricklayers Arms Junction on 11 September. The 09.02 Epsom Downs–London Bridge 4-SUB unit, No. 4704, collided almost head on with an ECS working hauled by No. 33041 from London Bridge at the end of the new reversible line from Spa Road. The driver of the latter had brought his train to a halt after seeing the approaching EMU, but not soon enough to avoid the collision. He had mistakenly passed a danger signal believing a subsidiary position light signal was exhibiting a proceed aspect. The driver of the EMU and about forty passengers were injured. The cranes from Hither Green and Stewarts Lane cleared the site during the day. Members of the press blamed the working of the new signal box for the accident, but without having any evidence.

On 4 October a tank wagon on the 06.25 Salfords–Fawley freight train derailed near Swanwick and struck a passing DEMU, No. 1129. Luckily no one was hurt, although the driver suffered from shock.

Unusual Workings

On three consecutive days in February, the Ford Motor Co. chartered a train to take dealers from Victoria to Chichester to witness the unveiling of a new car. The train was made up of No. 73001 hauling eight mainly first-class carriages on 12 February and No. 73004 on the following two days.

Work on the M23 was coming to an end, which meant fewer trains of stone from Westbury were needed. Class 47s could still be seen on the Brighton line serving Salfords and Ardingly.

The quick thinking of a train driver between Tonbridge and Tunbridge Wells may have averted a serious accident when he reported signs of movement of the earth near Somerhill Tunnel. An earth slip then occurred that blocked the line, but the driver of the following train, having been warned, was able to stop in time.

On 29 March, No. 74007 arrived at Waterloo in charge of two 4-TC units, working as the 14.38 Weymouth–Waterloo. It often failed on arrival and was not able to operate the 17.46 return to Bournemouth, which had to be cancelled.

On 19 April, No. 35028 *Clan Line* worked light engine from Ashford to Hereford via Redhill, Guildford and Reading.

The longest train for many years appeared on the Central Division on 24 August, when a return excursion from Edinburgh to Chichester via Haywards Heath was double-headed by Nos 33051 and 33036, pulling sixteen coaches.

Another exceptionally long train, although not planned, was on 7 August near Herne Bay, when a failed Class 47 with eleven coaches on an excursion was rescued by a following 4-BEP/4-CEP, which pushed the stricken train to Faversham.

Two Class 20s, Nos 20146/80, arrived at Eastleigh from the north on a freight and returned soon after, also on a freight train.

Closures

Burnetts Lane Siding, between Eastleigh and Botley, was taken out of service. It served an Admiralty depot, which closed on 5 January.

The signal box at Salfords closed and was demolished, with access to the sidings being transferred to Earlswood.

Aldershot lost its freight facilities on 6 October.

Miscellanea

A list of lines was published over which steam traction would be allowed during the year. Unfortunately for the Southern, out of the twenty-three stretches of line cleared for steam running, only two were on the Region and these were Basingstoke–Salisbury (36 miles) and Eastleigh–Romsey–Salisbury–Westbury (43 miles). Twenty-two steam locomotives were cleared to run these specials, with No. 35028 *Clan Line* being the only Southern representative.

Mountfield Tunnel on the Hastings line had to close for about six weeks from February because heavy rain had damaged the brick lining. The track through the tunnel was singled and laid on a 9-inch-thick layer of concrete that covered the width of the tunnel. This was then covered with another 6-inch layer of concrete with the rails being fixed directly to it. Trains to Hastings were re-routed via Ashford and Rye and ran through to Bexhill.

By the start of the year all the new REP and TC units had been delivered and were in service. Many units were not in their proper formations when originally delivered and some coaches needed switching between units to create correct formations. More high-speed brake tests were carried out using REP No. 3009 between Woking and Basingstoke during April.

The 8-VAB unit was converted at Eastleigh and emerged as two 4-VEP units, Nos 7741/2.

In previous years, excursions from the region had been marketed under the name of 'Pleasure Seekers' and had been very well supported, but due to a shortage of guards and drivers, there had been none advertised early in 1975. It was April before the first one ran – a weekend trip from Brighton to Aberystwyth – and a week later another one ran from Eastbourne and Hastings to Spalding.

The spring bank holiday saw an upsurge in the numbers of inter-regional workings, with thirteen Class 47s and three Class 33s providing the motive power.

Class 47s could also be seen working Freightliner trains from Southampton to Crewe, Bescot and Stratford. They were also frequent visitors to the APCM works in North Kent with coal trains from Welbeck Colliery, many of which were double-headed. The occasional Class 45 also appeared on these workings. The empty wagons were then taken to Betteshanger Colliery where they were loaded and returned to the Midlands.

Although the numbers of Class 52s were diminishing, they were still being used to work stone trains from Westbury to Botley and Fareham.

In April, Eastleigh held another open day. Visitors were able to access a pit and walk under a DEMU. On display were Freightliner wagons and a Class 52, No. 1023 *Western Fusilier*, but the star of the show was David Shepherd's 9F, No. 92203, which arrived on an excursion from Westbury.

On 7 June a section of track between Lewes and Glynde subsided while contractors were working on drainage installations. Replacement bus services struggled to cope with the demand, especially as one of the trains affected was the Newcastle–Eastbourne and Hastings service, which was stuck in Lewes station. Many of the passengers and their cases were de-trained and pointed in the direction of the queue for buses. Eventually the Class 33 in charge of the train was uncoupled and ran round its train, having to go northwards to Cooksbridge to do so. It then retraced the route as far as Redhill, where it ran round its train again and proceeded via Tonbridge and Ashford, reaching Hastings from the other direction four hours late.

A 4-CEP, No. 7153, was refurbished at Eastleigh. Among the alterations undertaken were both MBS guard's vans removed and passenger windows fitted, new driver's entrance doors located behind the cab and all seating altered to Mk II standards. False ceilings with strip lighting were also installed. The two guard's vans in the MBS were replaced with a single one in the TC, which kept its first-class seating but lost its second class.

Weymouth was by now just a shadow of its former self. The sidings that had only been laid around 1960 to cope with tomato traffic had been lifted. The sidings leading to the goods shed had been lifted and a car park covered the area. The land that was once occupied by the motive power depot had been developed into a small housing estate. Some old station buildings still survived and they continued to be lit by gas. The only freight over the line was the tank car trains that operated three times a week to serve the ferries.

Although the Western Region DMUs were welcomed to help out the DEMUs of the Southern on the Portsmouth Harbour–Bristol services, they were found to be much slower, and the timetable between the two cities suffered.

The last 'Ladies Only' compartment disappeared when 4-SUB No. 4720 was taken out of service for modifications.

The first merry-go-round train from the South Western Division started in October, when coal unloaded from the River Itchen Wharves at Southampton was taken to Didcot.

Eighteen colour light signals were brought into use between Haslemere and Petersfield, which meant the end of semaphore signalling on the Waterloo–Portsmouth line. Petersfield Signal Box was modernised, but boxes at Liphook and Liss were closed.

A new signal box was opened at Petersfield.

3H Berkshire unit No. 1130, seen at Reading prior to starting off for Basingstoke.

On 3 May 1975, 3H Berkshire unit No. 1131 traversed the Weymouth tramway on an enthusiasts' special, the Dorset Dawdler, which started at Southampton and ended at Eastleigh. (Courtesy James Winnen)

Another view of the Dorset Dawdler railtour at Weymouth. (Courtesy James Winnen)

An unidentified Class 74 heads through Eastleigh on 20 April 1975 with the Up Ocean Liner express from Southampton Docks. (Courtesy Trevor Tupper)

4-SUB No. 4131 had motor coaches that dated back to 1939. It was photographed at Crystal Palace Low Level on a service from Victoria to West Croydon.

4-EPB No. 5116 is seen at London Bridge on a service from Charing Cross to Hayes via Lewisham.

A view of Cannon Street with three 4-EPB units in view. No. 5345, on the left, is about to depart for Hayes via Lewisham.

A 2-EPB, No. 5675, stops at Denmark Hill. It was one of a batch of thirty-four introduced in 1953.

Hampshire 3H unit No. 1125 heads another 3H at Bramley with a Basingstoke to Reading train on 19 August 1975. (Courtesy Kevin Lane)

2HAP No. 6093 leaves Gillingham in August 1975, bound for Cannon Street. (Courtesy Kevin Lane)

4-CIG No. 7425 calls at North Sheen on a Waterloo–Reading via Richmond service. (Courtesy Kevin Lane)

Chapter 7

1976

London Termini

The new signalling scheme at London Bridge was brought into use on 20 April. In order to do this, Charing Cross, Waterloo (Eastern) and Cannon Street stations had to be closed. Disruption was kept to a minimum by carrying out the changes overnight.

Waterloo had some preliminary improvements made to it as well. The barriers on the concourse and the old departure boards dating back to 1922 were put up for sale. The old clock, the rendezvous point of thousands of people, would survive the alterations.

Industrial Action

1976 did not bring an improvement in industrial relations, with unofficial strike action taking place throughout the year. On Monday 2 February there was a 24-hour unofficial walkout by drivers at Farnham, Guildford and Effingham Junction, who were protesting at revised duties. This affected services badly on the Alton line, Waterloo–Guildford via Cobham and via Ascot and Aldershot.

Some guards stopped work for fifteen minutes on 1 March in remembrance of one of their colleagues, who had become involved in an incident with a passenger and later died.

29 June saw more industrial action taken by drivers at Waterloo, which led to the cancellation of 600 trains. The strike was in response to how one of their members had been treated at a disciplinary hearing.

Another strike hit the Salisbury area on 5 August. This dispute was over which depot should supply the crew for a special train.

Fratton drivers withdrew their labour at weekends at the end of November. This was because some drivers' hours had to be altered to cope with scheduled engineering works.

Accidents

On 14 May, 2-SAP No. 5917 became derailed at Staines. It was not in service at the time, and so there were no injuries.

An unusual and serious accident occurred overnight on 9/10 August. A ballast train with a locomotive at either end set off for Idsworth, between Petersfield and Rowlands Castle. On reaching the site the train divided, with the front portion then going on to Rowlands Castle. The rear portion was left on a falling gradient and it ran away and caught up with the, by then, stationary front portion, smashing the

2-SAP No. 5917, seen derailed at Staines on 14 May 1976.

4-EPB No. 5146 became derailed as it entered Cannon Street on 29 April 1976.

brake van and tool van as well as derailing the track-laying machine. Several of the crew were injured and had to be taken to hospital. The damage did not end there, as the breakdown crane that had come from Wimbledon to clear the line toppled over and blocked the Up line.

Later that month, on the 19th, empty stock that was being moved from Platform 4 to the Up sidings at Guildford collided with the rear of the 17.54 Waterloo–Portsmouth Harbour train. Three coaches were badly damaged and a number of passengers were injured.

Two Mermaid ballast wagons derailed on points just south of Orpington on 4 September. They had run for some distance off the tracks and caused damage to both track and the Chelsfield Up platform.

At Lewes, the junction at Southerham Junction where the Newhaven and Seaford lines leave the Eastbourne line was re-sited nearer the town. This meant that the signal box controlling the junction could be closed as the new point work was controlled from Lewes box. But on 15 June, within just a few weeks of the track being altered, a 4-CIG, No. 7303, on the 18.44 Brighton–Ore service derailed while going over the new junction, completely destroying it. The train was signalled correctly through the junction on the Down main line and approached the junction under power at between 35 and 40 mph. Sometime after the leading coach had passed over the correctly facing points, the point motors started to operate under the second coach and the trailing bogie of this coach struck the partially open points and was diverted onto the branch line. This caused the second coach to slew sideways out of line until its rear bogie was forced into derailment and dragged across the junction, seriously damaging the switch diamonds. The third and fourth coaches were similarly dragged into derailment. The points had been free to move because the signalman on duty at Lewes had rendered the interlocking inoperative by the irregular use of a release key. Five passengers were injured and the signalman collapsed while being interviewed but later recovered. Straight track was laid after the unit had been cleared from the site, allowing services to Eastbourne to run, but Newhaven trains could not recommence until a replacement junction could be re-laid.

Two DEMUs were damaged at Tunbridge Wells Central when they joined up violently. A number of passengers were injured.

Towards the end of the year, there was a terrible spate of accidents involving pedestrians or passengers. One man was injured when he fell from a train near Charing Cross, a sailor fell on to a live rail at Margate and was killed, a lady had both legs amputated when she fell under a train at Dartford, and a boy was killed when struck by a train while trespassing between Brixton and Victoria.

Unusual Workings

A railtour using a Hastings 6B unit travelled over three freight-only lines on 1 May. These were to Ardingly, Beeding and Lavant.

A Class 31, No. 31230, was again on Royal Train duties, picking up the President of Brazil at Gatwick and taking him to Victoria for a state visit.

Another Class 31, No. 31257, was used to haul the Royal Train from Waterloo to Ascot for the Derby on 2 June.

Class 52s continued to be visitors to the Region, taking freights to Norwood Yard. On 26 March, No. 1051 *Western Ambassador* derailed in the yard, blocking it for some time. Towards the end of the year, though, these duties were increasingly worked by Class 50s.

Closures

The independent goods line between West Croydon and Waddon Marsh was taken out of service on 1 February. This line had run parallel with the electrified West Croydon–Wimbledon line and had served the industrial complex around Waddon Marsh and Beddington Lane. Most of the sidings there had already been lifted and the only freight that used the line was an occasional oil train from Fawley. These invariably entered the site from the Wimbledon end. 1975 had seen the final workings over the Merton Abbey line and the junction at Merton Park had already been removed. The electrified lines were closed in 1997 and the route is now part of the Croydon Tramlink.

At Wareham, the two bay platforms that served the Swanage line were taken out of service on 5 May. A couple of weeks later, Worgret Junction Signal Box, which controlled the junction for the Swanage branch, was closed. Furzebrook Sidings were by then controlled from Wareham.

Ashurst Signal Box on the Oxted line was taken out of service on 8 July.

Crossing boxes at Mortlake and White Hart Lane were taken out of service on 5 and 19 December respectively, with their crossings being monitored by CCTV and controlled from Barnes.

Miscellanea

The Waterloo & City line re-opened after the November flooding on 12 January.

The 1970s was the era when the IRA were very active and bomb scares were fairly frequent. On 18 February, a bomb was reported to be on Charing Cross station at about 19.00. Luckily, it turned out to be a hoax. On 4 March, however, at about 08.30, a bomb did go off on a 4-EPB unit, No. 5343, but luckily it was ECS being removed from Cannon Street. The explosion occurred at Borough Market Junction, causing substantial damage and injuring passengers on a train passing in the other direction. The damaged carriage was subsequently removed and it ran for a while as a 3-EPB unit.

A briefcase was left in a toilet on the 20.10 Charing Cross–Dover train on 21 March. This was suspected to be a bomb and the train was evacuated at Orpington. It was subsequently discovered to be a harmless briefcase with papers belonging to a student.

Charing Cross was closed for a while on 29 March so that a suspect device could be removed, and further down the line the 17.14 Cannon Street–Ramsgate was held at Herne Bay while another suspicious package was removed. These were by no means the only closures and delays caused by suspect devices.

The Southampton–Portsmouth service had run virtually competition free as there had been no regular bus services between the cities. However, the M27 had opened and a new bus service marketed as 'the Solenter' had been introduced, and although it took ten minutes longer – one hour compared to fifty minutes – it was seen as serious competition to already declining passenger numbers. The Hantsway services faced further competition later in the year when another private bus service started between Southampton and Salisbury, which only took ten minutes longer than the train. Reliability of the train service was not great as the Western Region trains arriving at Portsmouth were so late that they left out many of the smaller stations on the return trips in an effort to pick up time. The service was so bad that a petition was raised by passengers complaining about it. The 15.19 from Bristol to Portsmouth Harbour had only been on time on five occasions out of sixty-six during May, June and July.

On 11 March passengers on the 17.36 Victoria–Uckfield and East Grinstead service had an exciting if hairy ride. Their train consisted of three DEMUs. The jumper cable between the first and middle units parted, which rendered the brakes and lights on the rear six carriages inoperative. The train accelerated down the 1 in 100 incline after Lime Siding and failed to stop at Oxted station. It sped across the viaduct before the driver could bring it to a halt in Limpsfield Tunnel. The signalman at Oxted had given the 'train running away' signal to the next box, Hurst Green. Staff from Oxted arrived and escorted the train back to the station, where the jumpers were re-attached, and the East Grinstead portion continued its journey.

There were cuts to some services in a bid to cut losses. From 20 April on the South Western Division eighteen trains into and sixteen trains out of Waterloo were axed. These were all suburban services. The Central Division suffered even more cuts, with main line services to the coast as well as local services being cut. This meant that the use of 4-SUBs diminished appreciably.

Southampton made it to the Cup Final, playing Manchester United at Wembley. Two football specials ran, one headed by a Class 47 and the other double-headed by Class 33s.

During May tests were carried out, with No. 33010 being given permission to run at 85 mph. Other tests involved the two HAPs that were not converted to SAPs (Nos 6022/3) undergoing trials using the new 'Tightlock Coupler'. They were attached to test coach *Hermes*.

The Seaspeed hovercraft service ceased running on 1 May between Southampton and Cowes, which was the last Seaspeed service on the Solent. The service continued though, operated by the British Hovercraft Corporation. The Hants & Dorset bus that took passengers from the hovercraft terminal to Southampton station bearing an all-over advert for Seaspeed also disappeared and was replaced by a private operator.

Woolston tip closed in June after a life of twenty-two years. On opening ballast trains stopped between Bitterne and Woolston and the wagons' contents were discharged down the embankment. As the tip grew, sidings were laid that were controlled by a ground frame. In its heyday, two trains arrived every day carrying station and engineers' waste. The contractors working the tip had their own 0-4-0 WD diesel shunting locomotive. In later years, only one train each day arrived at the tip. On closure the Region's waste was taken to a tip at Farnham.

Brighton open day was staged again for the first time in two years with the usual exhibits being brought from Lovers Walk sheds, including No. 34051 *Winston*

Churchill and No. 30850 *Lord Nelson*. Also on display was the modernised 4-CEP No. 7153. Trips to the old goods yard were not allowed as the track had been deemed unsuitable for passenger use, but No. 73122, working on its diesel engine, pulled driving trailers from No. 7780 full of enthusiasts to Lovers Walk, where more exhibits were on display.

Chart Leacon held its own open day on 21/22 August. An hourly shuttle service was run to the works by 3-D unit No. 1318. Visitors were informed that Class 71s were all due to be withdrawn from service.

Excursion trains were proving to be very popular, especially on the South Eastern Division, which witnessed twenty-eight such trains during late June and July. Most of these were worked through by Class 47s, but some emanating from the LMR electrified lines changed motive power in the London area and Class 33s took over. Locomotives working through from other Regions invariably had to work light from resorts to Chart Leacon to refuel for the return trip. Specials leaving the area proved a problem as there was a shortage of suitable loco-hauled rolling stock, so this had to be brought in from the Central or South Western Divisions or even from other Regions.

The Central Division resorts of Bognor, Brighton, Eastbourne and Hastings saw an upturn of excursions arriving over the previous couple of years. Eastbourne continued to be reached via Ashford and Hastings, which meant that Class 33s rather than 47s had to be used. One of the longest excursions to run left Hove on 19 November on its way to Aberdeen. It was called 'The Granite City'. It needed double-heading as far as Willesden by Nos 33049 and 33065 as it consisted of thirteen coaches. It returned on 21 November.

On 1 July, No. 74007 was in charge of the Weymouth Quay to Waterloo service. At Winchester, the cab of the loco started to fill with fumes. Passengers were detrained, but the driver managed to take the train to a siding that was accessible to the fire brigade. The driver was overcome by fumes doing this, but recovered later.

Many people still remember the long, hot summer of 1976, possibly because of the disruption it caused. There were many lineside fires, even though steam had ended, and buckled rails led to delays and cancellations.

All Class 71s were taken out of service on 3 October, with their duties being covered by Class 73s. They were to be stored for two years, and if no work had come available for them, they would be scrapped.

Attempts were made to keep the tracks clear of leaves on the line with three water cannon: No. 001 was based at Guildford, No. 002 at Chart Leacon and No. 003 at Dover.

Christmas mail traffic continued to decline and EMUs were only needed for parcels work for two weeks rather than the usual three.

The sight of milk trains at London termini came to an end during the summer. Platform 15 at Waterloo was used to turn around the milk train, which left Clapham Yard at 09.36 and went to Vauxhall, where it discharged its load. From there it went to Waterloo, where another loco attached to the rear and took it back to Clapham.

There was a daily delivery to United Dairies' creamery and bottling plant at Vauxhall. The train would come from Torrington. It would have to be divided at Clapham Junction so it did not foul other running lines while unloading.

There is lots of roof detail evident on this shot of Dover Marine as No. 09013 shunts its train on 15 May 1976. (Courtesy Stuart Ray)

Two Hastings gauge Class 33s, Nos 33202 and 33203 (formerly D6587/8), were parked at Tonbridge on 15 May 1976. (Courtesy Stuart Ray)

Class 71 No. 71010, formerly E5010, is seen at Tonbridge on 15 May 1976. (Courtesy Stuart Ray)

Class 73 No. 73111, formerly E6017, is seen at Stewarts Lane on 15 May 1976. It was withdrawn in May 1991 and scrapped six years later. (Courtesy Stuart Ray)

Also at Stewarts Lane on the same day as the previous image was MLV No. 68005. (Courtesy Stuart Ray)

The Up Night Ferry heads through Brixton with No. 71011 in charge. The service lasted until 1980. (Courtesy Kevin Lane)

4-TC No. 424 is seen at Waterloo during August 1976. (Courtesy Hugh Llewellyn)

The sidings at Wimbledon hosted a 2-HAP, No. 6002, which had been introduced in 1957, and a 4-SUB, No. 4294, which dated back to the 1940s.

Still in green livery, Class 47 No. 47366 heads through Clapham Junction with a freight for Northfleet Cement Works in Kent. (Courtesy Kevin Lane)

Chapter 8

1977

London Termini

The old arrivals boards and Windsor lines departure boards at Waterloo were demolished by the start of the year, but the main line departure board remained in use until 17 July, when it was replaced with a new Solari indicator, which came in three parts. The main board spanned the entrance to Platforms 12 to 15, which showed

This was the old departure board for the Windsor lines at Waterloo station. (Courtesy Kevin Lane)

all departures and main line arrivals. Two smaller boards, one of which was over Platforms 3 to 6, showed departures from Platforms 1 to 15, while the other was over the Windsor line platforms and showed departures from Platforms 16 to 21. The old departures board was saved and was taken to the National Railway Museum at York.

Naval Review at Spithead

This event took place during 25 to 28 June, with the Royal visit taking place on the last day. Visitors were asked not to travel to Portsmouth in their cars, but rather to use public transport. On the Sunday extra trains ran between Portsmouth and Southampton, but on the Tuesday there were extra trains to/from Waterloo, Brighton and Eastbourne. Five trains left Waterloo for Portsmouth or Southampton. Extra trains were on standby, including two eight-car EMUs at Fratton and Portsmouth with a DEMU at Portsmouth & Southsea. An 8TC with a Class 33/1 was also stationed at Fratton.

Industrial Action

The start of the year had seen an improvement in industrial relations, but on 19 May drivers at Norwood staged a lightning strike lasting 24 hours when they walked out in support of one of their fellow drivers who had been sacked for being drunk on duty. It was mainly freight services that were affected.

Signalmen at Gillingham also walked out in support of one of their members who had been disciplined for 'gross signalling irregularities and failure to observe safety rules'. The strike spread to Swanley, Maidstone, Faversham and London Bridge. Talks with union hierarchy and promises of an appeal meant that the signalmen resumed their duties, but not before some unfortunate passengers had been stranded for over four hours.

It was not only rail workers' actions that led to cancellations and delays. In November a power workers' dispute led to voltage reductions to the railway, which caused signalling and track circuit failures, and in some cases total blackouts in station buildings.

Accidents

On 29 January eight loaded tank cars jumped the tracks at Southcote Junction, which led to the suspension of all services between Basingstoke and Reading for two days.

Another freight train that jumped the track was on 4 March at Plumpton when the 11.54 Norwood–Eastbourne derailed. Most of the wagons were loaded coal trucks but an oil tanker was involved and the fire brigade attended as a precaution. The accident also severed power cables that cut off power to Falmer and Newhaven, causing much disruption.

At Borough Market Junction on 6 May the 04.14 Addiscombe–Cannon Street ten-car EMU derailed while crossing between the Up Charing Cross and Up Fast Cannon Street. The trailing bogie of the second motor coach of No. 5039 derailed and was ripped from the bodywork. The coupling broke, causing the 2-EPB behind, No. 5735, to also derail, blocking the Up Charing Cross. It was left overhanging Borough Market after first demolishing the wall that had been rebuilt only the previous weekend after a similar accident in 1970! The wheels became derailed as the stock rail had been raised by the insertion of a half sole plate on the last sleeper before the points, for which a track gang had to bear full responsibility.

No. 33043 was one of the two Class 33s involved in an accident at Mottingham on 11 July 1977. The other one, No. 33036, finished up at the bottom of an embankment. (Courtesy Peter Beyer)

On 3 August a collision occurred near New Cross, where two Down lines converge into one. One train had passed a signal at danger, and when its driver realised another train was overtaking him, it was too late for him to stop. The two trains collided, tearing a bogie from each. Five passengers were hospitalised but were released after treatment. The signal in question, L207, had been passed at danger twice in 1976 and again soon after this accident. The enquiry concluded that:

> L207 is easily seen from a good distance although it is to the right of the line around a curve when it first comes into view. Signals L215 and L221 first appear to be to its left and are thus seen before L207 as the eyes search right-handed. Whereas L207 stands against the sky as a background, the other two have a hill behind them, a factor on a bright day. I conclude therefore that the reason Driver Newington drove his train past Signal L207 at danger was that he 'read through' and accepted the Green aspects in Signals L215 and L221 as applying to his train, and he took Signal L209 as his also. I believe that this also applied to the other drivers concerned in the incidents referred to in this report.

On 11 October a coal train that had derailed near Mottingham was hit by a double-headed cement tanker train. The loco, No. 33036, and several wagons overturned and slid down the embankment, coming to rest in several back gardens. The other loco, No. 33043, suffered severe damage to the cab. The line was closed for three days while the track was cleared of debris. The cement from the full tankers had to be pumped out into lorries and taken away by road. No. 33036 was not recovered until the end of November, when two cranes lifted it from the bottom of the bank.

A large number of cement tankers also overturned and had to have their contents pumped out.

Unusual Workings

A football special ran from Brighton to Oxford on 22 January and consisted of No. 33043 hauling eleven coaches, which included a buffet and a first-class Pullman, formally *Hawk*. If the fans thought they could travel in style, though, they were wrong, because this was reserved for the directors and players! The Pullman was also used by the team for away games at Rotherham and York.

The PEP units went to the Technical Centre at Derby on 7 January. They returned a month later and were assigned to Wimbledon. The three units, which had been the first to use sliding doors, had to work in eight or ten-car formations as they were not compatible with any other coaching stock. The two-car unit had been withdrawn in August 1974 and the two four-car units were officially withdrawn from service in May 1977, but they continued to be used by the research department. The 2-PEP was fitted with a new coach that was equipped with a pantograph, was reclassified as a Class 920 and was renumbered 920001. It was used in the development of the Class 313/315s. The two four-car units became Class 935 and were renumbered 056/7. The former had little use before it was transferred to Derby in 1980, whereas No. 057 was used as a testbed for new bogies between 1979 and 1983.

A railtour celebrating ten years of the Bournemouth electrification took place on 10 July with a trip from Waterloo that took in Surbiton, Guildford, Havant, Southampton, Bournemouth, Salisbury and Weymouth. Motive power was shared by Class 74s and Class 33s.

On 19 February, Class 52 No. 1013 *Western Ranger* operated a railtour that left Waterloo and traversed a route that this class had never been seen on before as it visited Southampton, Weymouth, Netley, Havant, Guildford, Reading and Staines before returning to Waterloo.

Two EPB units traversed the Hastings–Ashford line on Sunday 3 April, hauled by No. 33040. The reason for this was that they had undergone some work at St Leonards and were needed back in London, but the lines at both Plumpton and Burgess Hill were closed for engineering works.

On 6 October No. 47159 failed at Wallers Ash while working a Freightliner from Southampton Maritime. It was assisted to Basingstoke by the following train – a 4-REP on a Weymouth–Waterloo service.

A Class 31, No. 31294, made it into Brighton on 15 October after deputising for failed No. 33210 at Salisbury on an Exeter–Brighton service.

Closures

The Poole–Wimborne freight line closed on 2 May. In its last days it only saw two freight trains each week, on Tuesdays and Fridays. Its closure was marked by three specials on 1 May from Bournemouth using TC stock.

In early April, Aldershot B box was decommissioned with Aldershot A becoming just Aldershot. The remaining semaphore signals were replaced with colour lights.

Miscellanea

By the start of the year the Lymington branch was being worked as 'One Train Only' from Lymington Junction Box on the main Bournemouth Line and from 16 January more savings were made by abolishing the ground frame at Lymington Pier and demolishing the Down and Up home and Down distant signals. The level crossing was downgraded to an unmanned crossing worked by the user.

The Hastings diesel units that had been working the Saturdays-only trip from Brighton to Exeter were needed to work a more frequent service from Charing Cross to Hastings, so the journey reverted to being loco-hauled. The coaching stock for this trip was brought from Yeovil on Friday night and returned to Clapham Yard on Saturday evening. The last DEMU on the service ran on 30 April.

The Portsmouth–Bristol service was also put back to being loco-hauled and driver training was taking place during February. Class 31s were in charge of the bulk of these services, although Class 33s were often used owing to loco failures. One of these failures was within the first two weeks of the service, when the heating boiler on No. 31209 exploded between Porchester and Cosham. The blaze needed the fire service to attend but there were no injuries. A week after that another Class 31 ran out of fuel at Romsey. The service had been the subject of many complaints of overcrowding and the lack of toilet facilities since the DEMUs took over the service in 1973.

The Brighton football specials continued to run with very little trouble, thanks partly to the stewards who patrolled the train, but when Portsmouth's fans visited Brighton on 6 April, trouble started in the afternoon on the 12.52 Portsmouth Harbour–Brighton, with hooligans threatening both passengers and crew. At Barnham, normal passengers were taken off and the train continued non-stop to Hove, where police were waiting. The two following services were disrupted but to a lesser extent, and the returning special was wrecked. Three 4-CEP units, Nos 7137/74/93, had curtains ripped down, seats slashed and bulbs smashed. Items including tables, fire extinguishers and cushions were thrown from the train. At one level crossing a car waiting had its windscreen smashed by a corridor handrail that was thrown from the train.

Portsmouth fans led to more delays on 17 September after losing at home. The communication cord was pulled on the 16.56 Portsmouth Harbour–Bristol soon after the train left Fratton. Supporters then jumped from the train onto the track, requiring the power to be switched off. When the train eventually arrived at Cosham, the police ejected some of the troublemakers.

A new freight service commenced in April, taking cars from Sheerness Dockyard to Liverpool and Stranraer.

Inter-regional and inter-divisional specials continued to thrive, with seventy-eight being reported in the Eastern Division during late May and June. This included nine trains from Liverpool Lime Street to Dover taking football fans on the first leg of their journey to Rome for a cup tie. This caused problems for the Southern as only Class 33s were allowed from Mitre Bridge Junction in West London. This was because drivers from Norwood had not been trained to drive Class 47s – they were to do so later in the year. Stock was dispersed at various sites before returning to Dover to take the fans home northwards.

Autumn and leaves on the line were causing their annual problems. Water cannon Nos 001 and 002 were being used on the South Western Division around Milford, Haslemere, Cobham, Camberley, Guildford, Redhill and Ascot. Despite their best efforts there was a shortage of stock due to flat tyres caused by skidding.

A new de-icing unit, No. 004, was formed from coaches from No. 4361 and allocated to Fratton. This replaced No. 017, which was withdrawn. Two more units, Nos 005 and 006, were converted at Selhurst from Nos 4380 and 4126.

An open day was held at Ashford on 16 July. Among the exhibits were Nos 08414, 33208 and 73131, as well as No. 73119, which was attached to a breakdown crane and demonstrated the re-railing of a goods wagon. 2-H No. 1119 operated a shuttle service from Ashford station and the works.

The open day at Brighton took place again. This year the newly restored 2-BIL No. 2090 was used to take enthusiasts to Preston Park. A couple of Brighton Belle motor coaches, both from No. 3053, were on display. These had been brought back from Essex by a private purchaser. Two of the usual exhibits were missing – Q1 No. 33001, which was by then at the Bluebell Railway, and No. 34051, which was considered too shabby for public display.

From October Mk II coaching stock ousted the older Mk I carriages on the Waterloo–Exeter services.

No. 74003 was captured at Lymington Pier while operating a farewell tour to the Class 74s on 3 December 1977. (Courtesy Arnie Furniss)

The Class 74 Farewell Tour arrives back at Waterloo to be greeted by a host of photographers. (Courtesy Arnie Furniss)

No. 33109 about to propel its train out of Bournemouth Central station. (Courtesy Ian Nolan)

MLV No. 68001 leaves Victoria bound for a Channel port – either Dover or Folkestone. The units could work with electric stock or on their own using battery power over un-electrified lines on docks.

A very wet day did not deter this photographer from snapping No. 74005 at Southampton Central.

Hasting 6L unit No. 1037 rounds the bend at Tonbridge on its way to the South Coast. (Courtesy Kevin Lane)

Chapter 9

1978

London Bridge

The work on the terminal part of London Bridge was completed and opened by Sir Peter Parker, Chairman of BR, on 15 December. Work was still continuing on the Eastern side. He also announced a £200 million programme of improvements to the Region over the next ten years. This would include refurbishment and the replacement of stock on the Western Division.

Industrial Action

It was 12 April before any industrial action caused disruption in 1978. Drivers at Waterloo staged a 24-hour stoppage in support of one of their members who had been disciplined.

The NUR had instructed its members not to train any new staff in learning their jobs. Management got round this by attaching brake vans to Class 33 or 73s, with new staff being taught by inspectors riding in there rather than in cabs with the driver.

A one-hour strike took place at Feltham panel box on 7 June between 13.00 and 14.00, causing delays and cancellations to Windsor and Reading services.

Guards, or a lack of them, could also bring services to a halt. This happened at Gillingham on 18 June at 21.00. A Grove Park guard had been asked to work a duty normally covered by a colleague from Victoria, but as it entailed a trip on the Sheerness branch, which he was not familiar with, he refused. He informed his control of this and was instructed to carry on, but again refused to do so. Other guards at Gillingham walked out in support of him.

Guards flexed their muscles again at six London depots and Horsham on 20 September. They walked out to show their disapproval over controllers taking over trains when actual guards were not available.

Southern drivers threatened to strike every Wednesday from 22 November in support of a pay claim to receive a bonus equal to that given to pay-train guards. Western Division drivers started their action a week earlier, causing thousands of cancellations.

Accidents

On 10 February, a de-icing train derailed at Tonbridge and hit a bridge, damaging both train and bridge. Luckily, the crew escaped injury.

Five 4-VEPs were damaged in an accident on 30 March when a train of ECS ran away from Woking towards West Byfleet. The driver had left his two 4-VEP units, which had terminated there, but used an incorrect method to apply the brakes when leaving his cab. Another relief driver was due to reverse it from the platform to sidings, so when the train started moving, he assumed that this was what was

This image shows the damaged sustained by the two units involved in the fatal crash near Patcham on 19 December 1978.

happening. However, a signalman noticed that this was not the case; rather, that the train had no driver and was rolling away. Both the staff at Byfleet – the next station, and where the train was heading – and emergency services were informed. At Byfleet, the 09.12 Waterloo–Basingstoke and Alton was held at the platform and all passengers detrained before the runaway train smashed into it. Despite this three passengers and the driver sustained minor injuries and substantial damage was done to both units.

On 8 September the 08.10 from Guildford derailed as it entered Platform 14 at Waterloo when the rear bogie of the seventh carriage, 2-SAP No. 5904, jumped the tracks at a facing crossover. A subsequent enquiry found that the track was worn and poorly maintained. There were no injuries but signal cables were severed and it caused much disruption. Eight trains were stuck between Waterloo and Vauxhall and power had to be turned off to allow 5,000 passengers to be detrained.

Several cows were killed on 20 September between Grove Ferry and Minster when they wandered through a gate that had been left open and onto the track. They were struck by 4-CEP No. 7151, which derailed after the impact.

The most serious accident of the year occurred during the evening of 19 December. The 21.20 Victoria–Brighton had been halted at a signal north of Patcham Tunnel because a person had fallen onto the line at Brighton and power had been turned off while they were rescued. The following train, the 21.40 Victoria–Littlehampton service, passed a signal at amber, but failed to slow significantly. It is thought that the next signal, which should have been showing red, was not lit and the train continued at speed. By the time the driver saw the stationary train in front of him and made an emergency brake application it was too late, and it hit the stationary train while still travelling at 45 to 50 mph. Of the following train, the 22.29 Haywards Heath–Brighton, the rear portion that had detached from the train in front at Haywards Heath had also ran past the broken 'red' signal, but was able to stop when the driver saw the red blinds of the train in front. Three people died including the driver of the 21.40. Damage to both units was substantial and clearing the tracks was hampered by the units being jammed beneath a farm overbridge. The line did not re-open until 23 December.

Another fatality occurred at Milford level crossing when a train overran a red signal and hit a car. The motorist died instantly.

Unusual Workings

An Italian Speno track-grinding machine, complete with Italian crew, visited the Region in January. The Swiss-designed train consisted of five four-wheeled coaches painted bright yellow and included living accommodation for the crew. When in action, the amount of sparks it produced was so great that neighbourhoods were warned beforehand that it was coming to allay any fears and reduce 999 calls.

Another unusual train to visit the Region was an ultra-sonic test train, DB97500/8.

February saw delays due to bad weather, with conductor rails icing over. On 16 February it was particularly bad in the Alton, Guildford and Reading areas.

Class 33s were called into action to rescue stranded electric units and it was reported that a train arrived at Alton at 09.00 consisting of twenty-two carriages made up of several stranded trains.

A Class 73 headed the 07.27 Eastbourne–London Bridge train, consisting of 8-CIG, because an EMU driver could not be found. The loco was taken from a freight service.

The unusual sight of a Deltic in Sussex and Kent occurred on 26 March when No. 55007 *Pinza* worked an enthusiasts' special from Victoria to Dover via Gillingham and Canterbury, returning via Ashford to London Bridge. It then continued to Bognor Regis. No. 73127 then pulled the train to Littlehampton, where *Pinza* took over again, returning to Victoria via Hove.

Two enthusiasts' specials ran over the Fawley branch, the first from Totton using a 3-H DEMU on 23 April and on 22 July when a 6-D from Waterloo visited. It was the last passenger train to use the station as the station buildings were demolished soon after to make way for improved access to the refinery sidings. Passenger services had finished over the line in 1966.

Football specials carrying Brighton fans continued to run and they were now adorned by a headboard reading 'The Seagulls Special'. The first-class Pullman, E314E, which had been used on previous trips, was still attached to some of these trains for the exclusive use of players and officials.

Unusually, a Class 73, No. 73123, was in charge of the Royal Train to the Derby. The same loco was used to take the President of Romania from Gatwick to Victoria six days later. The Prince of Wales was only given a 4-VEG to travel in, but this did not stop one television reporter from calling it a 'high-speed train'.

A Class 40 on an excursion arrived at Hastings via Ashford and Rye. Class 47s were still barred from this route but 40s had been cleared.

The Spastics Society (now Scope) had an exhibition train and on 6 October this travelled behind No. 33023 from Portsmouth to Brighton. The Duchess of Kent was on board for part of the journey.

Other exhibition trains to visit were the Rovex carrying 'Hornby Early Bird Express' headboards. It visited Bromley North on 4 November, arriving from Salisbury. It left the next day to Kensington (Olympia).

On 17 November a 'Stiff Records Exhibition Train' arrived at Margate from Oxford, leaving the next day for Guildford. Stiff Records were a record label specialising in punk bands and gigs were played at towns visited.

Closures

The signal box at Gatwick Airport was taken out of use on 26 April with its working being taken over by the Three Bridges box. This box also took over the functions of Balcombe Tunnel box from October.

Star Lane Signal Box on the Quarry Line was also officially taken out of service. It had not been used for a number of years as it only controlled a siding to a sub-station and a crossover, which was unused, clipped and padlocked. The box had been fire damaged for about a year and was probably unusable anyway.

The revised track layout at Brockenhurst installed during October meant that the signal boxes, Brockenhurst 'B' and Lymington Junction, were taken out of use. Brockenhurst 'A' became Brockenhurst. The connection for Lymington Pier at Lymington Junction was taken out with the single branch line running parallel with the main line from Brockenhurst.

Miscellanea

The Pleasure Seekers Club that ran several excursions had to apologise to its members over the lack of buffet facilities. This was because the Southern only had one buffet car that could be used on trains from other regions.

Kent's three coal mines were still in production, with three daily trains running from Betteshanger and Shepherdswell. There had been no rail traffic from Snowdown although the mine's steam locomotives were still in active service.

At Southampton Docks, although much of the past trade had diminished drastically, volumes of car imports/exports had increased with Leylands and Datsuns being the mainstay. All shunting on the docks had been in the hands of Class 08s, with all dock traffic entering and leaving via the Western Docks entrance at Millbrook. Boat train traffic to the Eastern Docks had virtually dried up and the crossing boxes at Chapel and Canute Road were only manned on an 'as required' basis.

Two letters appeared in *The Times* during April. The first, from the Chief Passenger Manager, revealed that BR was exploring the possibility of re-opening the Blackfriars–Farringdon tunnel and extending some services to West Hampstead, where a full-scale interchange was envisaged with Metropolitan, Midland and North London trains. The other letter was not as upbeat as it stated that to cut costs on the proposed Channel Tunnel, it would be only a single track. Additionally, the idea of new high-speed tracks through Kent had been dropped.

Conversions were undertaken at Selhurst to units Nos 7788–99. These were given increased luggage space and were used solely on the Gatwick Airport service. They were re-numbered 7901–12 and re-classified 4-VEG (Vestibule Electro Gatwick) and branded 'Rapid City Link Gatwick–London' on an orange stripe applied immediately below the roofline. This branding was later moved to beneath the driver's cab window. The BR branding of 'Arrows of Indecision' was accompanied by an aircraft symbol.

Senior citizens who held a Railcard were given free rides across the system on 10 June, and despite extra trains being laid on from Waterloo to Portsmouth, Southampton and Exeter, overcrowding was still reported. The Central Division was also struggling to cope with the extra traffic. An 8-EPB made it as far south as Eastbourne. Matters were not helped when a ballast train reversing at Coulsdon North hit two 100-ton tankers, which ran away and demolished a set of buffers at the Purley end of a siding. One of the wagons overturned, blocking the Down fast line. The fire brigade were summoned and, fearing an explosion, ordered the power to be turned off and evacuated the area. It was three hours before the slow lines were re-opened to traffic. If this was not bad enough the lack of a signalman at Worthing caused the box to be closed for over two hours. It was reported that one train – the 14.10 Victoria–Brighton – travelled via Mitcham Junction, Dorking and Horsham to Littlehampton. On arrival there it found the lines through Worthing shut so it retraced its steps to Horsham, then to Three Bridges, and then down the main line to Brighton, arriving a mere five hours late!

A shortage of moquette meant that some units were outshopped with older styles of seating material, and one unit, No. 6151, appeared trimmed with material used on some pre-war buses.

Two more de-icing units were converted using 4-SUB carriages. These were numbered 007 and 008, with the former being nicknamed *Icefinger*.

Bob Dylan held a concert at Blackbushe Airport on 15 July and an estimated 250,000 fans turned up, 40,000 of which arrived by rail to Fleet station. They came in thirteen special trains that left Waterloo between 06.54 and 12.24. Most of these were ten-car trains made up of HAP units that provided high seating capacity. Other specials ran between Basingstoke and Reading.

At Feltham permission was given to build a new container terminal on the site of the old goods yard and motive power depot. It would take up 18 acres, which was about a third of the site, with the rest being used for housing.

The new football season saw football fans not being content with throwing items from trains. On 5 August, after a 'friendly' at Fratton Park, three youths were thrown from the 17.30 Portsmouth–Southampton train as it was leaving Fareham. One of these youths fell under the train and received serious injuries.

A cup tie match away at Nottingham on 13 December needed four special trains to convey the fans, but all did not go well. The first train, which was carrying the team, had left at 08.57. This was held up by a locomotive failure in the Leicester area and arrived two hours late. Two of the following supporters' trains, all pulled by Class 33s, were not so lucky. They were delayed behind a failed Class 45 near Elstree and did not arrive at their destination until the match was virtually over. They were taken straight back home again and it was a credit to the Brighton supporters that the trains arrived back undamaged.

From August, any vehicles not fitted with continuous brakes were barred from the Central Division.

The Grain–Hoo Junction branch was busier than in the days when it was open to passenger traffic. Up to twelve trains every day were needed to serve the oil refinery and traffic was also derived from the Marinex Gravel Co. at Grain. Very little evidence remained over the whole branch that it had once served passenger traffic.

On the Isle of Wight, some of the old Southern station buildings had been demolished and replaced by bus shelter-type buildings. Brading still retained its original buildings and even its gas lighting.

An explosion took place at West Croydon on 22 September when a store hut caught fire. Gas cylinders stored inside exploded spectacularly, shattering glass in station buildings and damaging nearby cars, causing the surrounding area to be evacuated.

Brighton drivers were trained to drive Class 47s, as were drivers from Redhill and Norwood depots.

New freight workings were introduced, bringing stone from Westbury to help with new sea defences at Deal. Delays were caused to services though as several trains headed by Class 47s had slipped to a halt between Dover and Martin Mill and assistance had to be obtained by banking from the rear. This was in the form of a Class 33 or 73 that was attached at Ashford before proceeding.

No. 07010, formerly D2994, was at Eastleigh during February 1978. It is now preserved at the Avon Valley Railway. (Courtesy J. Woolley)

No. 33010 trundles along beside the man with the red flag at Weymouth during August 1978. (Courtesy Neill Instrall)

No. 73101 was seen at Reading during March 1978. (Courtesy J. Woolley)

Class 33 No. 33118 and 4-TC No. 432 are seen at Weymouth in August 1978. (Courtesy Neil Instrall)

A WR Class 119 DMU, No. B585, ventures into Southern territory near Weymouth in August 1978.

An unidentified Class 33 waits at Weymouth Quay during August. The '90' head code shows it is about to start off for Waterloo. (Courtesy Neil Instrall)

A view of the yard at Guildford with an unidentified Class 73 on shunting duties. (Courtesy Kevin Lane)

Brading was one of the last stations to retain gas lighting, which it kept until 1985. The passing loop was lifted in 1988.

Chapter 10

1979

London Termini

Platforms 1, 2 and 3 at Charing Cross were closed from May to September while the old wrought-iron girders of Hungerford Bridge beneath the wooden floor were replaced by steel ones. 400 trains each day used it, carrying 24,000 passengers. The bridge occupied the site of Brunel's original pedestrian suspension bridge and was built in 1863 after plans to widen the original bridge to carry trains were dropped. Some Hastings and suburban services were diverted to Cannon Street and Blackfriars or terminated at Waterloo East.

At Victoria track alterations to the Eastern side were finished in August and work started on the Central side, which was expected to last until the middle of 1980. The work involved the closure of some sidings and some trains terminated at Clapham Junction. New ticket barriers were also installed.

Channel Tunnel

The idea of a Channel Tunnel was revived by BR. It would still consist of a single line under the sea. This scheme would use existing lines from London and the plan to build a huge marshalling yard at Cheriton was dropped, with a new yard at Neasden proposed as a replacement. There would also be freight facilities at Ashford. In all, the scheme would cost £650 million. Up to ten trains would run in one direction and then ten would return. It was forecast that the tunnel could be operational by 1990 and would carry 8 million passengers and 8 million tonnes of freight by the end of the century.

Brighton Line Resignalling

A £45 million re-signalling scheme for the Brighton line was announced. The scheme, which had the backing of the government, would give the line the most modern equipment available. The plan only involved renewing signalling as far north as Norwood Junction, because the line from there to London Bridge had been updated in 1976 and a scheme to Victoria was already under way, and was due for completion in 1983. Work on the whole line was due for completion in 1987. Only two signal boxes would be needed to control the whole line, with a new box being built at Three Bridges that would make thirty-three smaller boxes redundant. The entire line would be fitted with welded rail and equipped with AWS (advanced warning system).

Industrial Action

It was not long into the new year before long-suffering passengers were hit with more industrial action. On 3 January guards working on 4-SUB units refused to work them because there was ice on the wooden step boards, making them unsafe to use.

On 10 January members of ASLEF, the train drivers' union, on the Western Division unofficially withdrew their labour before the official strikes organised for the 16th, 18th, 23th and 25th of the month. The last day caused most disruption as there were no de-icing trains running, causing more misery for passengers the following day.

Accidents

A Hastings DEMU, No. 1032, crashed into the buffer stops at Charing Cross on 11 January. It had only just been returned from Swindon Works after a major overhaul.

The cab of 6L No. 1032 after crashing through the buffers at Charing Cross on 11 January 1979. (Courtesy Peter Beyer)

The view of the same accident from the opposite direction, showing how far past the buffers the unit went. (Courtesy Peter Beyer)

Two trains collided at Hampton Court Junction on 23 February. These were the 12.20 Alton–Waterloo and the 13.13 Hampton Court–Waterloo. The latter had just left Thames Ditton station and passed the branch signal at danger and was entering the Up slow line when it struck the sixth carriage of the passing eight-coach Alton train made up of 4-VEP No. 7708 and 4-CIG No. 7423. The leading car of the errant unit, No. 4662, was derailed. It slid down an embankment while No. 7423 lost a

Two of 4-SUB No. 4662's coaches came to rest at a crazy angle after being hit by 4-CIG No. 7423 at Hampton Court Junction on 23 February 1979. (Courtesy Peter Beyer)

bogie. The rear two cars of the Alton train demolished a brick parapet of a road bridge. Thirty ambulances attended the scene but fortunately those requiring hospital treatment were numbered in single figures.

A fatal accident occurred at Hilsea on the night of 24/25 February. The 01.35 Eastleigh–Portsmouth & Southsea, which consisted of No. 33115 hauling 4TC No. 414, struck the rear of a crane that formed part of an engineers' train while

Another view of the 4-SUB, No. 4662, after sliding down the bank. (Courtesy Peter Beyer)

travelling through green lights. The cab of the diesel was extensively damaged and unfortunately the guard who was travelling in the cab was killed. Five passengers and four other railwaymen were injured. At the time the engineers only had possession of the Up line, but the crane was on the Down line.

The conclusions of the investigation into the accident did not attribute blame to a single person. They found there was not a competent person in charge of the operation and that all of the staff were inexperienced. They also found that taking possession of only one track for the task in hand was impracticable. There were also failures attributed to the staff at Portsmouth Signal Box.

A derailment of a train of empty oil tanks at Clapham Junction on 3 February caused chaos. It derailed at the southern end of the station as it left the West London line and blocked both the Up and Down slow lines, damaging track and signal cables.

On 27 August a special from Feniton to Margate was shunted into a siding already occupied by a twelve-car electric train. These units were pushed back into the buffer stops, causing damage to both. The locomotive, No. 47342, and the adjacent coach were damaged after becoming buffer locked. No. 47145 brought another rake of rolling stock to Margate to take the trippers home.

Unusual Workings

Class 50 No. 50016 from Barham worked over the Oxted line on 7 April when it was in charge of a railtour from Paddington to East Grinstead. It also ran to Horsham, Guildford and Redhill.

Another unusual sight was No. 73136 and 4TC No. 415, at Seaford and Newhaven Harbour on a special visiting Sussex branches on 31 March. The Ardingly branch was deemed unfit for passenger workings, although Class 47s still used it on aggregate trains.

A charter train carrying the headboard 'The Fall and Rise of The Pines Express' was run to Bournemouth and Weymouth on 13 May. Motive power was double-headed by Class 31s Nos 31135 and 31304.

A 4-BEP, No. 7017, was used on Royal duties on 31 May to take Her Majesty from Victoria to Lewes, and then from Brighton back to London. A week later, though, on her annual trip to the Derby, the Royal Train was used, being hauled by No. 73142. The same motive power was used a week later to take the President of Kenya from Gatwick to the Capital. The loco was kept in pristine condition until August, when it was again used on Royal Train duties to take the Queen Mother from Portsmouth Harbour to Waterloo, and a week later when it took the Queen from Waterloo to Southampton Western Docks.

Four exhibition trains visited the Region during 1979. A Phillips Data Systems Exhibition train visited Maidstone East and Bromley South during June. It was brought from Slough behind No. 47225 and left for Marylebone behind No. 33060.

Another exhibition train to visit Maidstone was representing Lever Brothers. It arrived from Marylebone behind No. 33204 on 20 July. Travellers Fare, who provided refreshments to rail travellers, celebrated their centenary with an exhibition train that toured the country. On 19/20 September it arrived at Fratton from Paddington, then visited Weymouth and Southampton before moving on to Cardiff.

'Joinery on the Move' was another exhibition train that visited during September.

Four specials were needed to take Nottingham Forest football fans to Channel Ports on their way to a European cup tie with Malmö in Munich. All were hauled by Class 47s.

No. 47238 worked the 08.01 East Grinstead–London Bridge on 18 September and was the first of its class to work a scheduled passenger service over the Oxted lines.

One of the 4-PEP units, No. 4002, returned from Derby in APT livery, and during October was used on test runs between Basingstoke and Woking.

Closures

Winchester Junction Signal Box officially closed on 25 March, but its sole function had been to operate the single line token instrument to Arlesford after the panel box had opened at Eastleigh in 1966. It is doubtful whether it had been used after the Mid-Hants line closed in February 1973.

Victoria East Signal Box closed on 13 May, with its duties being transferred to the new panel in Victoria Central.

Hampton Court Crossing Box was abolished on 29 July when the lifting barriers came under the control of Surbiton Panel Box.

Miscellanea

The year did not start well, with snow and ice covering the whole Region. On the Western Division, there was no through service between Waterloo and Weymouth until 8 January. Semi-fast trains did reach Bournemouth, however, from where a shuttle service to Weymouth operated. Passengers could not understand the reason for this as it had not snowed for a couple of days. On 4 January notices were displayed saying that the disruption was caused by snow entering the traction units of many units, rendering them inoperable.

More snow fell on 23 January, causing more chaos. It led to one unusual sight. Two electric trains became stuck early in the morning on the Staines to Waterloo line. One train was stuck at Feltham and another at Ashford. The following train was a Class 37, No. 37215, with a load of tankers being taken from Ripple Lane to Earley. It left its train in a siding at Feltham and collected the two stranded EMUs – which were made up of one 4-EPB and four 2-EPBs – and took them to Twickenham, where it was detached, leaving them to continue under their own power before returning to its own train.

On the Central Division, things were no better. Trains were arriving at Victoria up to two hours late. The station was jammed with trains, many of which were stuck because their crews were still on trains trying to get into the station. Another strange formation caused by the weather was a Victoria–Brighton train made up of an 8-SAP headed by Nos 31114 and 73002.

The South Eastern Division did not escape the chaos either. On 14 February four Up trains became stuck on Sole Street Bank on the Chatham route for up to nine hours. It took six hours to free the first two, which then continued to London. The rear two were eventually hauled back to Rochester by diesels. A BR spokesman apologised for the delays, stating that they did not realise how bad things were and that they had expected the trains to free themselves. About 2,000 commuters were stuck on the trains without refreshments, heat, or, for some, toilet facilities. One person stuck was Divisional Manager Bob Newlyn, but he did not make his position known to his fellow travellers.

The cold snap lasted into February and Class 33s, and in some cases Class 09s, were stationed throughout the region to assist stranded electric units. To try to placate passengers, a pamphlet was produced explaining the problems that snow and ice created on the electrified lines, outlining the detailed steps that were being taken to alleviate the problem, but warning that there was no solution in sight.

Management must have judged the pamphlet a success as they issued another one, this time apologising for the state of the rolling stock. They assured passengers that changes were on the way with the introduction of new suburban line trains for services out of Waterloo. The refurbishment of all the Kent Coast stock would be completed in 1982. Similar work would then be undertaken on Brighton and Portsmouth line stock.

A third pamphlet was produced later in the year explaining the problems caused by leaves on the line.

The world's first all concrete cable-stayed bridge was opened by Sir Peter Parker on 7 February. It carried the Staines–Weybridge line over the M25. While it was being built a new line was laid around the bridge during the two years it took to construct. The lines were then re-laid on their original route.

A new service was introduced between Brighton and Manchester. There were two trains in either direction on weekdays and one on Sundays during the summer, but on winter Sundays the train started and finished at Gatwick Airport.

A fire broke out at Victoria station on 4CEP No. 7130. It spread to all four coaches of the unit and to sister unit No. 7210 on an adjacent platform, which also suffered damage. No. 7132, which was coupled to No. 7130, was also damaged superficially and 4VEP No. 7856, on another adjacent platform, suffered smoke damage.

Another fire broke out at Victoria on 1 March. Again fire spread from one train to another at an adjacent platform. It started on the 20.40 to Ramsgate and spread to the 20.44 to Dover Marine.

Yet another fire broke out on a 4-CEP, this time while it was on the move. Luckily it was late at night and there were only two passengers on board. It broke out at Seasalter between Whitstable and Faversham on the front coach of No. 7149. It rapidly spread to the next two carriages and four fire engines were needed to put the flames out.

The Faversham–Canterbury East route was due to be closed over the weekend of 28/29 April in order for a new bridge to be rolled into place over the Canterbury bypass. Unfortunately, one of the embankments had subsided and the bridge was found to be 10 feet too short! This meant that the line was closed until 8 May, when remedial work could be done and the bridge could be installed.

Mini timetables for each route were introduced and were given away for free. A million were printed at a cost of £85,000.

The first of the Class 508s, built at York for suburban services, was delivered during August. No. 508001 was delivered to Strawberry Hill on 9 August, with the next six units being delivered by the end of September. Crew training started during September on the Shepperton branch. The first revenue-earning service for a Class 508 was on 17 December when an eight-car train ran from Waterloo to Hampton Court and Shepperton.

Four new DEMUs classified as 3Ts or 204s were built using two-car Hampshire Class 205s with the driving trailers of ex-EPB previously used on Class 206 Tadpole units placed in the middle. The cabs of these were permanently locked. They were numbered 1401–4 and were based at Eastleigh for use on Hampshire, Wiltshire and Berkshire services. Their introduction did not go totally smoothly as a minor fire broke out in No. 1401 and No. 1404 was involved in a minor collision with No. 6062 at Portsmouth Harbour.

Brighton lost its allocation of 4-CEP units, Nos 7101–12, to Ramsgate to cover units that were being refurbished at Swindon and the ones that had been damaged in fires. This left the Central Division short of stock but this was addressed by four peak hour services from Brighton to London being run using Class 73s hauling eight Mk I carriages. The units were returned in October and loco-hauled services to London ceased.

The Chipman Chemical Company's weed-killing train was used across the region again. In the past it had used one locomotive on a push-pull basis; this year, however, crews refused to propel the unit as they claimed they could be affected by the chemical spraying them, so a locomotive was needed at either end so that it could always be driven from the front.

There was a national oil shortage during the summer, and although most services were unaffected, being electric-hauled, DEMU services throughout the region faced cuts. This shortage affected the number of excursions entering the Region and their numbers fell sharply.

A shortage of guards continued to cause cancellations on the Eastern Division, and it actually seemed to be newsworthy that a female guard had been spotted at Maidstone East, but this rare sighting had not been verified! It was proving impossible to recruit new staff to many positions even though there were over a million people unemployed.

There was an unusual reason for delays on the line through Balham on 14 August. A crane working on the line overnight had its jib stuck in the 'up' position and it could not be moved because there were bridges either side of it. All trains had to be diverted via the slow line or via Crystal Palace.

Class 56s were first seen in the Eastern Division from August when they appeared on Blue Circle (APCM) coal trains to Northfleet.

Despite all the problems mentioned, and hundreds more minor ones, the punctuality rate was generally not too bad. In August 153,416 trains ran and over 140,000 of these, or 91.4 per cent, were on time or under five minutes late. The following month this dropped to 90.2 per cent. In October, however, the Central Division sunk to a low of 64.1 per cent mainly due to problems at Victoria. Across the Division in October there were fifteen point failures and thirty-eight signal failures.

On a lighter note, a consignment of mice escaped from the brake van of 4-CIG No. 7350. It was thought that they had all been re-captured, but on 5 November the unit had to be taken out of service due to complaints of smell and further sightings. Sixteen more were re-captured by 7 November.

4-EPB No. 5112, introduced in the early 1950s, waits to leave Hampton Court on a trip to Waterloo during May 1979. (Courtesy Neil Instrall)

Class 33 No. 33005 waits beneath the signal gantry at Cardiff prior to working a passenger train to Portsmouth.

Class 31s took over the running of the Bristol–Portsmouth service in 1977 and No. 31211 was photographed at Warminster in May 1979.

Another Class 31 near Salisbury on a Portsmouth–Bristol service in July 1979.

4-VEC No. 045 is seen at Ryde during August 1979. These units were converted at Stewarts Lane from 1920s Metro-Cammell Underground stock. (Courtesy Neil Instrall)

Double-headed Class 73s Nos 73110 and 73115 head a coal train from Betteshanger in Kent through Acton Wells Junction. (Courtesy Kevin Lane)

4-VEC No. 044 is seen at Ryde Pier Head in August 1979. (Courtesy Neil Instrall)